A game of marbles on South Main in Trenton, Kentucky at the turn of the century.

Images of the Past

TODD COUNTY · KENTUCKY

PICTORIAL HISTORY

Volume II

TURNER PUBLISHING COMPANY

Easter Egg Hunt at the Trenton Baptist Church. From left: J.C. (Teddy) Woodall, David Joiner, Lewis (Tink) Bransford, Charlie Payne

Turner®

PUBLISHING COMPANY

Turner Publishing Company
Publishers of America's History

Publishing Consultant: Keith R. Steele
Project Editor: Charlotte Haris

Library of Congress Catalog Card No: 2003114844
ISBN: 978-1-68162-578-2
LIMITED EDITION

TABLE OF CONTENTS

PREFACE

*"To look backward for a while is to refresh the eye, to restore it,
and to render it more fit for its prime function of looking forward."*
-Margaret Fairless Barber

Silver Triangle Main Street is pleased to present the *Pictorial History of Todd County Volume II*. As a newly chartered organization, we earnestly want to extend our hope for the future of this community with each of you. We are honored to be involved with this reflective publication. It has certainly been a vexing, yet rewarding experience. Contributions of time and effort toward this goal abounded. Each of you should feel proud of your legacy in print. We would like to thank everyone involved.

The repsonse was overwhelming, however, therein lies the problem. With photograph submissions in excess of one thousand, many donations were omitted. For each disappointment, we are truly sorry. We can offer hope that with its' success, this book will spawn future publications. Perhaps one day a truly comprehensive collection of pictorial volumes will be enjoyed by our descendants.

We deeply appreciate the generosity exhibited in sharing your family's memories. We hope that this compilation will provide an interesting and entertaining glimpse at what makes this community special. I offer special thanks to the promotions committee members who labored diligently on this project. I must also extend my deepest gratitude to my mom for her devotion to seeing it through.

It is the wish of Silver Triangle Main Street that you may enjoy this look back in time as much as we did compiling it. May reflection draw us all together in pursuit of a better tomorrow!

Chris Cole
Promotions Committee Chairman
Silver Triangle Main Street
September 3, 2003

TODD COUNTY PICTORIAL HISTORY BOOK
VOLUME II COMMITTEE
2003

Tracy Fournier
Silver Triangle Main Street Director

Chris Cole
Silver Triangle Board Member
Promotions Committee Chairman

Marcia Hines

Lelia Cole

PORTRAITS OF TODD COUNTY CHILDREN

Chester and Joe Stahl, 1901

Lucy Rebecca Fortson
June 8, 1912

Louise Hightower (Dill)

Lola Edwards

Brother and sister Frank Dillard (Dill) Payne and Carolyn Payne

Ann Showers Chesnut, born Nov. 23, 1879

Willie, left, born Sept. 26, 1902, and Ray born Sept. 1, 1900, sons of George Robert and Pearl Miller

Tom Lee and Minor Reasons, Guthrie, KY

Nora Mae Fox

Alice Miller Chesnut
1886

July 1926 - Pernie Miller McKeehan's children, John and Martha

Edith Edwards

Dorothy Dill (McIntosh) 1923

Martha Carolyn Payne, left, and brother, Frank Dillard (Dill) Payne

Mervin (left) and Albert Greenfield, 1921

Tommie(left) and Sarah Averitt

Anaise Fox, daughter of Tom Fox

Margretta (Gretta), left, and Annie Burge

From left: Jimmy Jones, Elizabeth Ann Jones, Ann Elizabeth (Boo) Payne, Sue Carolyn Payne and Elaine Ryals

From left: Jim Gower Glascock, Carolyn Payne and Charles Glascock

Grandchildren of George Robert and Pearl Miller. From left: Betty Katherine, Joe Wendell, Margaret Ophelia, and Grace Evelyn Miller, 1936

The oldest children of John and Jenny Fletcher Bond. Elzie, seated, Geneva and Wiley. Wiley later operated Bond Feed Mill on W. 3rd St. in Russellville, KY. Geneva graduated from Homer High School in 1930 and played on the girls' basketball team. Photo 1914

From left: Ben, Chester, and John Stahl, 1940

Nancy Glascock being pulled on sled by her dog

Tarleton Averitt, 1920

Hiram F. Dill, late 1940's

Charles Glascock, Carolyn Payne, and dog

Sue Carolyn Payne

Lorraine Gilliam (Chesnut), 1936

Frank Dillard (Dill) Payne

Girtie and J.W. Boyd

Future Hall of Famers, from left, brothers, Jerry and Spurlin Cobb on the Cobb farm, 1950

Billy and Joe Neale Fox

Ben (left) and John Stahl, 1940

From left: Pamela Allen, Jeff Burchett, Barbara Burchett (Rogers), Marcia Allen (Smith), 1954

Earl Ray Welborn, Jr., age 5, and Virginia Simpson Welborn, age 3, dressed as Indians with their little LEE dolls

Patie Wilkins (Dill), and Lela May Wilkins, 1918

Billie Payne Ryals and Charlie Payne on Billie Payne Ryals' tricycle

Neighbors and friends Billie Payne Ryals, left, and Martha Jo Rutledge

Billie Payne Ryals, age 2

Danny Lee Harrison, son of James Lee and Christine Harrison

Freddie Delany Harrison, son of James Lee and Christine Harrison

Joe Neale Fox

First cousins, from left: Lelia, John Smith, Kathleen, and little Mike Chastain on the event of Mike's first birthday, April 12, 1946

From left: Phyliss, Melissa, and Amy Killebrew, daughters of Lawrence and Kathleen Killebrew

Sisters Lelia Chastain (front), Edith (left) and Mary Chastain, 1940

J.W. and Jewell Boyd
October 1, 1937

Terry Michael Cole portrays
Davy Crockett in his Christmas
attire in 1956

Billy Fox

Double first cousins Lelia
Chastain (Cole), left, and Kathleen
Chastain (Killebrew), 1941

Gerald Barnett, current Chief of
Police of Elkton, KY, in 1947

Brothers Norman Lee Fox (left)
and Thomas Henry Fox

Alan (left) and Grant Dickinson,
1948

Jerry Cobb in the snow at Seays
Grocery, March 1960

Dalma Enola Martin, the first of five children of Claude and Lina
Hadden Martin, is shown with her toys at the family farm on Martin
Road off of Hadden Mill Road in north Todd County. Dalma died
December 24, 1917 at the age of seven.

From left: Nellie, Enols, Louisa, and Mabel Mason on the "Old
Charlie Wolfe Farm," circa 1932

PORTRAITS OF TODD COUNTY LADIES

Annie Burge (Payne)

Gertrude (Gertie) Payne

Ann Showers Chesnut 1879-1966

Suzy Seay, 1942

Ellen Breakfield, 1922, Allensville, KY

Martha Carolyn Payne (age 16)

Nannie Bryan Greenfield, Guthrie, KY, 1934

Miss Annie Nold Wells, Circuit Court Clerk, 1928-1964

Katie Lassiter Ryals drinking from a sulphur well

Lucy Fortson Chastain ready for a swim at Dunbar Cave swimming pool, 1940

Nannie Bryan Greenfield, Guthrie, KY, 1934

Louise Hightower (Dill). Louise was a telephone operator at Sharon Grove for many years. Married to Thelbert Dill

Vernell Nixon later married Willard Stratton, Elkton, Kentucky, 1945

Olive Maria Northington, wife of George Snadon, born 16 October 1866, died 19 January 1897

Nannie Bryan Greenfield, Guthrie, KY, 1934

Eula Poe, Elkton, 1945

Ann Elizabeth (Boo) Payne, 1953

Nellie Ruth Camp

Martha Carolyn Payne

Wedding dress of Emma Fox Welborn from 1895

Lucy F. Chastain while teaching in Mississippi, 1937

An eloquent lady of a century ago. Curlie Ada Brown (1879-1905), mother of Mrs. Floyd Orange, Russellville and the late Buna Ray Brown. Photo taken 1895

Susan Frances Weatherford, wife of John Franklin Snadon, born 13 April 1841, died 31 January 1920 in Guthrie

Mide Deason Mitchell of Allegre, late 1800's

Opha Addison Boyd, Sept. 1921

Carol McElwain Allen

Lotice Marion Smith, 1922

Esther Campbell Wyatt

Adie Mae Taylor, Trenton, KY

Dorothy Payne, owner and operator of Dorothy's Beauty Salon, Trenton, for many years

Louise Mayer, Guthrie, KY

PORTRAITS OF TODD COUNTY GENTLEMEN

John Franklin Snadon, born 22 October 1826 died 14 September 1889 in Todd County

George Snadon, born 7 August 1866, died 1 August 1929. He was Mayor of Guthrie in 1902 and was Treasurer of the Planters' Protective Association.

George Snadon, Grand Marshall of a parade held in Guthrie, perhaps a reunion of the Planters' Protective Association

Frank Dabney Snadon, son of George Snadon and Olive Northington, born 7 February 1888, died 20 May 1967

John McAfee Chastain, 1924

Kent Greenfield with the New York Giants

Felix Bryan in the 1940's

M.V. Lyon's campaign card for county judge, 1905

Hiram F. Dill, 1957 (1936-1988)

E.S. Hurst during construction of the Trenton Gymnasium in 1937

Isaac Euel Wyatt

Norman Fox, George Fox's grandfather. Norman was a Todd County magistrate.

William Hugh Ryals, Paris, TN. Picture taken in his study

Frank Dillard (Buck) Payne, Sr.

County Judge R. N. Cartwright, 1942

Governor Wendell Ford and James M. Groves, Circuit Court Clerk, Todd County

George Snadon, Jr., born in Rockingham County, Virginia, in 1798, married 1 September 1823 in Todd County, Sarah Jane Cross, daughter of John Cross and Lucy Tomlinson. He died in Todd County, 20 September 1883. His father, George Snadon, born in Augusta County, Virginia, in 1756, came to Todd County about 1812 and died in 1820.

Bobby Gene Allen, 1946

Burnice Wilkins, 1927

Howard Dorris, Guthrie, KY, married Nannie Greenfield

Shelton Dickinson, Trenton, KY

The Todd County Four sang at churches for years - John Phillips, Lee Glenn, Paul Phillips, Glenn Wyatt

1973, Guthrie Boy Scout Troop #182 Eagle Court - David Moore and Mark Fowler

COUPLES

George Robert Miller and Inez Pearl (Robey) Miller, married Dec. 19, 1895. Parents of Ray and Willie Miller

Ann Showers Chesnut with son, Ike Chesnut, 1904

Joseph Lee and Maggie Gorrell at their home near Claymour

Johnie E. and Mary Elizabeth Heltsley Wilkins, early 1900's

Virgil and Edna Harrison, newly married

George and Ovie (Hall) Harrison

Dorothy and Robert (Bob) Payne in front of their home in Trenton, KY

Martha Elizabeth Adams and Rainey Moore

Edwin C. Farmer and wife Nellie Johnson Farmer at the Farmer home on Cemetery Rd, Trenton, 1940

Daniel and Evie Powell Rager

Robbie Watts and Clifton Cobb in front of the Mt. Zion Baptist Church, 1942

Hiram M. Dill and sister Dorothy Dill (McIntosh), 1937

Claude E. and Lina Hadden Martin, circa 1940

Robert H. Rager and wife, Lula Mae (Wilkins) Rager, life long residents of Todd and Logan Counties. Parents of Bertha Rene (Rager) Dukes of Todd County

Nannie Bryan Greenfield and Howard Dorris, 1934

Felix and Ethel Bryan in 1942

Lelia and Sheridan Cole at the 50th Anniversary Celebration of the Kentucky State Police in Louisville, KY

B. M. Coursey and wife, Pearl Lyon Coursey, 1960

Felix and Ethel Bryan in the early 1940's

Christmas 1960. Mrs. Joe (Sue) Brown and her dad, Jim Spencer. Sue operated Sue's Beauty Shop for eighteen years in Sharon Grove and her dad was a partner with his son-in-law, Joe Brown in the Sharon Grove Feed Mill.

Marilyn Camp and Ed Radford at the underpass of the L&N Railroad in Trenton

Kathleen (left) and Lelia Chastain 1940 at Dunbar Cave

Lawrence and Kathleen Chastain Killebrew

Bobby and Pie Ware

Seymour and Ada Jane "Jennie" Heltsley. Ran a merchant store undertaker business in Clifty, KY, 1900-1920

John and Martha Stahl --King and Queen of the Todd County Sesquicentennial, 1971

Milam and Eleanor Chastain on a trip to visit their daughter, Marilyn King

Mary Elizabeth Heltsley Wilkins and Lue E. Heltsley Adams, early 1960's

Hiram M. and Patie Wilkins Dill, 1930

William "Johnnie" and Flossie Mae Bryant Ford, Clifty, KY. Parents of Helen Jean Williams, Kathy Gayle Starbird, Wilda Trent Harrison, Wanda Lynn Rice

Mack Chastain with first child, Edith, in 1930

Hiram and Patie Wilkins Dill, early 1960's

Marion Elliott and Patty Lawson Smith

Estelle and Albert Greenfield, Nov. 1944

Tintype of Margaret Russell and James Alexander Chesnut in 1851

Graham Cole with Uncle Sheridan, at Shelley Cole and Paul Haley's wedding

James Lee and Alice Christine (Kirkman) Harrison--Newly married (1948). Parents of Danny Lee and Freddie Delany Harrison

1954 - Murray State, Joan Bell and Bobby Phillips (became Mr. and Mrs.)

Billy W. Hogan (left) and Barry Cole at the waters edge at Paris Landing on Kentucky Lake, 1960

Chester, Sr. and Frances Stahl

Paul and Lucy Chastain, 1945

Bailey Mike and Lelia Rowena Chastain, at home in their front yard in 1945

FAMILY PHOTOGRAPHS

Front row, from left: John Henry Miller, Hester Walters Miller, Inez Robey, George Miller. Back row, from left: "Dink," "Mattie," "Pernie," Isabelle and Dru Miller.

Lower left: Gretta Burge. Upper right: Annie Burge

Gretta Burge (middle top step), Annie Burge (at Gretta's right) on the porch of the Burge home in Trenton

The Ferrell Brandon and Francis (Shepherd) Graham family of Trenton, KY area. Parents of lifelong resident of Todd County, Jack Leslie Graham. Photo taken circa 1900

Mary Watts, Eugene Oscar Watts, Elliott C. and Lucy Dickinson Watts at the home of Eugene D. and Lucy Watts. Circa 1922

From left: Robert Fortson, Lucy and Dunnie Fortson, 1925

Mrs. Fannie Sue Shelton Dorris (left) and sister, Mrs. Mary Elizabeth Shelton Glenn, with picture of their mother, Mrs. Mary Brown Shelton. 1950

Brothers and sister, from left: Dalton, Douglas, Minnie, and Theo Dickinson. Minnie married Dab Smith.

Will Dill and sisters, 1940's

James Lee and Christine Harrison with their first child, Freddie Delany Harrison

Miller-Coots family, 1938. Back row from left: Ray Miller, Etta Rea (Coots) Miller, Florence Coots, Ollie Mae Coots and Lucille Coots. Front: Grace Evelyn Miller holding family dog

Edward Smith family, front from left: Ellis, Edward, Kermit, Carroll Smith. Back row from left: Lotice (Chastain), Eleanor (Chastain), Alice (Kennedy), Hilda (Knepka), Lillian (Kennedy). 1948

A.E. Gant, with wife, Bell Lyon Gant. Standing: Romier and Iva Gant. Small Child in mother's lap is Leland Gant. 1901

John Carver family, 1918, from left: John, Nealy Dycus Carver, Clarence, and baby Bonnie Carver (Ewing)

From left: May Glenn, Virginia Glover and Agnes May Glover on the banks of West Fork Creek, 1919

Adults, from left: Richard Hogan, Mrs. Russell Hogan, Mr. Russell Hogan, Mr. and Mrs. H. H. Bellamy. Children: Karen and Billy Hogan. Easter Sunday at the Hogan Home

Mitchell family, 1911. Front, from left: George, Sam (father), Ivil (baby), Gilbert and Gillie (twins) Mide (mother) and Ola. Back, from left: Owen, Odis, and Omer. The twins were born June 1910.

Miller family - lady seated to the left is Hester Walters Miller, Elkton, KY

The Talmadge Moseley family, 1965 ad campaign gave the following 15 reasons to vote for Talmadge for Sheriff of Todd County. From left: Mary Jane, Mark, Charles, Kathy, Kenny, Pam, David, Andrew, Irene (mother), Baby William, Phillip, James, Thomas, Madge and Richard Moseley

24

The William and Lillian Sisk family. Top row, from left: George, Willie, Roberta, Maud, Nuet, Leon. Middle row from left: Martha, Roy, Bonnie, Marion. Bottom row from left: Evelen, Lillian (Grany), Juanita, William (Popa) and Paul

Front row, from left: Frank Camp, Warren Claytor, Joy Ryals, Jim Camp. Second row from left: Joy White Burge, Martha Camp, "Tish" Sarah Smith, Warfield Smith, Nancy Camp Reed, Maude Evelyn Claytor, James Rash Claytor, "Doc" Camp. Back row from left: Ernest Claytor, William Clay Camp, Cliff Camp, Lynn Burge, Jim Burge

Top row from left: Mervin Greenfield, Barney Miller and Albert Greenfield. Middle row: Robert Kirkman, Dennis Sears, Ora Greenfield Harris, Jesse Lee Miller, Irene Greenfield, Horace Harris, Estelle Greenfield, and Norene Harris. Children: Mary Bell Miller, Wilma Lee Miller, Eva Mae Miller, Billy Miller, Earlene Harris and Richard Greenfield, at the home of Horace and Ora Harris, 1948

Standing, from left: Barbara Camp, Cliff Camp, Marilyn Camp, Ann Ryals (first cousin). Seated from left: Mary White, June, Eloise Camp and Bobby Hall Camp (crying)

Back: Tony and Debbie Seay. Front, from left: Debbie, Brenda, and Patricia

From left: Ovie Lee (Hall) Harrison, George Harrison, James Lee Harrison, Roxie Lee (Wheeler) Harrison, Benjamin Emerson Harrison

Granny and grandchildren, 1930's. From left: Lucy Dickinson Watts, Richard Dickinson Jr., Georgia Watts, Virginia Reid Watts

Mason sisters, from left: Mabel Robertson, Enola Pena, Louise Randell and Nellie Sullivan, at the home of Thomas and Mabel Robertson on Pond River Rd.

From left: Margaret (Peg), R.E. (Coty), Katherine Ryals and Mary Ann Evans

Sisters-in-law on steps at Dunbar Cave, from left: Lotice Smith Chastain, Lucy Fortson Chastain, and Eleanor Smith Chastain, 1943

Hogan Bryan with grandsons, Hogan Bryan and Felix E. Bryan on the beach in Ft. Lauderdale, FL, in 1949-50

William Thomas Austin and son, Doug

A. E. Gant family. Front, from left: Leland Gant, wife, Nola, Iva Gant Ferren and son Paul Ferren. Back from left: Bell Gant, A.E. Gant, Essie Gant, and Romie Gant

Georgia M., Mina, Frank P., Frank Jr., and Dorothy C. Watts, 1927, Frank and Mina's home, Trenton

From left: Susie Pulley Robertson, Elsie Hurt Robertson and Lue Robertson standing in front of a 30 A Model Ford, 1945

Anaise and Martha Leigh Fox

Roxie Lee Wheeler Harrison with young boys, Freddie Delany and Danny Lee Harrison

From left: Milam, Paul and Mack Chastain

Samuel Farmer, Martha Jane Maynard Johnson and James Farmer, 1940

Sammy Porter holding daughter, Tracy Porter (Fournier)

Richard Hogan and son, Rusty

Estle W. Edwards, grandfather of Kathy Edwards Phillips and Paul Steven Edwards, 1958, Clifty, KY

Wilbur C. Cole and son Barry on the porch of the Cole home in Trenton, 1946

Pauline Cobb and sons, Jerry and Spurlin enjoying the cool water at Peachers Mill Creek, 1947

Lelia Rowena McAfee Chastain with new daughter-in-law, Lucy Fortson Chastain, 1939.

Bailey Mike and Rowena Chastain with new grandson, Mike, in 1945.

Novice S. Martin shown with his mother, Lina Hadden Martin. Photo taken circa 1934

Boley family: From left: Bernice, Willie, Nina (oldest girl), Lena, Damon, and Bessie Boley

Four generations, 1936: Mary Irene Dill (McGhee), Hiram M. Dill, Hattie Irene Taylor Dill, Margaret Ann Hooser Taylor Offutt

Front row from left: three little girls - Kathleen Johnson (Fletcher), Lola Johnson (Dawson), Eunice Johnson (Ewing). Second row from left: William Johnson Keatts, Nealy Spurlin Johnson, Ann Johnson, William Johnson, Betty Johnson (Hamby), Neavlean Johnson Taylor. Third row: Robert Johnson, Lewis Johnson, Ivy Spurlin, Edward Spurlin. Three generations, 1948

Brother and sisters, from left: Wilmoth, Ramie, Maude Evelyn, Annette, Lawrence, and Elizabeth Killebrew

Will Dill family, 1940's

Family of Daniel and Evie Powell Rager, from left: Ronald Rager, Margie, Bill, Evie, Mildred, Estelle, Edwin and Stella Edwards Rager, Melvin, Elise, and Dorothy.

The Jack and Verna Graham family taken at their home on Jeff Davis Highway. From left: Rebecca Shumate, Bobby Graham, Ricky Shumate, Susan Dukes, Brent Dukes, Jimmy Dukes, Linda Cowan, Mattie Graham, Karen Heflin, Elwood Graham, Debbie Holman, Jack Graham, Vicki and Verna Graham

Bruce and Opha Boyd sitting on the porch with a Mormon Elder and the children, J. W., Jewell, and Dorris Calvin Boyd

Lucy F. Chastain and son, Mike, in 1945

Martha Elizabeth Miller Fox

Sisters Lou McAfee Naive and Rowena McAfee Chastain, 1945

From left: Jerry, Pauline, and Spurlin Cobb, 1949

Warren Sanders family. Bottom from left: Mattie, Theresa, Warren. Top: Cherie

Four generations. Standing: Thomas Henry Fox (father of baby) Anaise Fox Small, son of Martha Elizabeth Miller Fox (holding the baby), and grandson of Hester Walters Miller (to the right)

Family outing to the Smokey Moutains at the Wonderland Hotel, 1947. From left: Sarah Payne, Mildred Van Meter and Barry Cole in the lap of Wilbur Cole, Lorraine Gilliam, Sheridan Cole. Back row from left: "Tootie" Cole, Bill Van Meter, Gladys Cole, Mac Cole, husband of "Tootie" and brother to Wilbur

Six of the nine children of Granville Newton and Virginia McKinney Hadden still living at the time this photo was taken in the mid 1950's. Seated, from left: Gill P. Hadden, Leon Hadden and Joe N. Hadden. Back row standing: Mrs. C. E. (Lina) Martin, Mrs. W. L. (Betty) Greer, and Mrs. M. W. (Ethel) Latham

From left: Lula Mammy, Ira Seay, Suzy Seay, Pauline Cobb, and baby Spurlin Cobb, 1942

Four generations of the Oscar Finney family in 1935. Front, from left: Minta Claire (Vernon), Carolina Gilmore (Mrs. Oscar). Back, from left: Orville Francis and father Mason. Carolina G. Finney was the mother of Mason and Georgia F. Stahl. Orville and Chester Stahl, Sr. were first cousins.

Chester B. Stahl, Sr., Todd County farmer and business man. Built and operated the Prescription Fertilizer Plant at Guthrie. Owned and operated the Guthrie Hardware Store. As a real estate agent he was instrumental in relocating to Todd County many families from what later became Kentucky Lake and Fort Campbell.

Front from left: Isabelle Adams Glascock, Frances Boyd. Back, from left: Betty Johnson, Ruth Edwards

Seated in front: Tip Jackson Shanklin and Georgia Anne Shanklin (brother/sister). Back, from left: Lucy, John, Will, Robert and Les Shanklin. Georgia Anne Shanklin was the wife of a Civil War veteran. 1940

Tarleton Averitt with great-grandchildren and his dog

Right: Back, from left: Lillian, Andrew, Robin, Raymond Chesnut. Front, from left: James Chesnut, Margaret Chestnut Barber, holding Tommy Barber, Ruth Chesnut and Janie Chesnut. July 1937

Mark Katherine Scott holding Tracy Porter

Roland and Martha Rust and their ten children in 1961. Seated from left: Naron, Peggy (Snyder), Martha, Roland, Nancy (Turner) and Malcolm. Second row from left: Ruth (Robertson), Lillian (Knowles) and Cynthia (Templeman). Third row, from left: Robert, Charles, and James. Children that are deceased: Naron, Peggy, Lillian, and Charles

FRIENDS

Martha Elizabeth Adams Luttrull and dog, "Bounce," at the homeplace

From left: Lorraine Gilliam, Sarah Payne, Gladys Cole, Mary Browder Smith, Sarah Van Meter, 1947

Lucy F. Chastain with her dog, at her home in Guthrie, Kentucky, 1943

Mr. G.W. Waller

From left: Dorothy Sue Lawson Sweeney, Ruth Edwards, Martha Elizabeth Adams Luttrull, circa 1930

Good friends, from left: Mary Alice Wright, Hazle Graves, Lucy Fortson, Mary Louise McClanahan, and Eugenia Scott in Guthrie, Kentucky, 1928

Childhood friends on Allensville Street in Elkton. From left: Marion Williams, Nancy Williams, Virginia Welborn, Jayne Cartwright, Louise Willis. Small child on ground Jean Landers. 1927

From left: Margaret Chesnut, Betsy Burrus and Mike Burrus with their pet kittens

From left: Lois C. Hill, Isabelle Miller Crawford, Viola Crawford

Traveling buddies, from left: Porter, Lotice Chastain, Mattie Clardy at Dallas-Fort Worth airport

Vernell Nixon and Flo Underwood, 1945

Nannie Bryan Greenfield, left, and Lucy Fortson in 1934, Guthrie, KY

Mary Payne, left, and Tula Thompson

Standing on Main Street in Trenton, from left: "Miss Annie" Hurst, Elva Dickinson, Katherine Patterson, and O. T. Evans (in back). 1937

From left: Nancy Bruce Adams Crouch (dressed in Indian costume), Frances Boyd, Martha Elizabeth Adams Luttrull, Isabelle Adams Glascock

MILITARY AND PUBLIC SERVANTS/POLITICS

Glover Williams, U.S. Navy 1940

Chester B. Stahl, Sr. U.S. Navy WWI, 1917

James Lee Harrison

Charles M. Breakfield 1923-1981, W.W. II Battle of the Bulge

William Webster Peters served in U.S. Navy during the Korean War.

Bruce Service, Specialist 4, US Army, 1959

Willis Camp, San Bernardino, CA, 1943

Joe Neale Fox

From left: Ida, Howard, and Ethel Dickinson

Congressman Ed Whitfield, Brig. General William Rutledge - Dedication of the Veterans' Memorial at the Court House in Elkton. In the rear is Ernest Wolff

REUNIONS

Dickinson family members, top row from left: Jess Dickinson, Jess Mather, Edlo Bacon. Middle row, from left: Douglas Dickinson, Dr. Howard Dickinson, Dick Dickinson, and Buck Dickinson. Bottom row from left: Grandmother Sara Dickinson, Walton Smith, Mary Dickinson, and Shelton Dickinson

An annual Dickinson family reunion

Trenton High School Reunion, Class of 1955. Bottom row, from left: Bobby Crouch, Mallie Smith, Sarah Averitt, Barbara Seay. Middle row, from left: Leslie Simmons, Shirley Simmons, Shirley Higgins, Lelia Chastain, Betsy Glascock. Top row, from left: Joe Henderson, Sonny Campbell, John Bartee, Sheridan Cole, Bobby Shackelford, Tom Bowman

Trenton High School Reunion, Class of 1945. Top row, from left: Larry Tribble, Bobby Watson, Warren Cornell, Herman Gilliam. Middle row: Martha Cox Hamn, Irene Luttrell Bates. Front row: Osie Stokes Clark, Sarah Payne Bouldin, Ned Glover, Bobbie Ann Woods McIntosh, and right front, Marie Brown Lewis, Dorothy Hyams Burney

Elkton family group. Front, from left: Glodine Petrie, Jacob Petrie, Anna Petrie, son and daughter of Michael. Back, from left: Michael and Lisa Petrie, Jason Petrie and son, Nicholas, Jack and Joyce Petrie, Denise, wife of Jason, and Shawn Petrie, son of Michael.

Class of '49, 50th Class Reunion. Front row, from left: Mai Church McCrery, Mayme Shanklin Clark, Earlene Mallory Hall, Dean Hadden Wells, Juanita Jo Harris Brabant, Nancy Dodd Murrey McElwain, Mary Belle Catron Noble. Back row, from left: Imogene Scott Short, Cynthia Rust Templeman, Chuck Gill, Marcia Dean Templeman Harris, Charles Cole, Margaret Thomas Everett, A.C. Statton, Patsy Short Showley, D. N. Short, Martha Averitt Rager, Earl Sears, Dorothy Petrie Sheppard, Rosella Wells Rager

WEDDINGS

Wiley Edward Brookshire and Nelle Grace Whetsel on their wedding day, November 18, 1948

Wedding picture of Ewing Farmer and Georgia Watts Farmer, 1943, standing beside the house of Georgia's parents, Mr. and Mrs. Frank P. Watts

Newly married couple, Flora Mae, and "Sweet Papa" Thompson leaving Mt. Zion Baptist Church in 1945

Rudolph and Gayle Cartwright Hall, married January 3, 1948, at the Elkton Baptist Church

Wedding photo of Earl Ray Welborn, Jr. and Sarah Catherine Haithcock on November 28, 1946

Clara Roush Bell married to Caleb Norris Bell circa 1905-06. She was from Oklahoma, where Mr. Bell met her while he was there in a cattle investment business. She was the mother of the late Caleb Norris, Jr. and Henry Roush Bell, all of whom are buried at Glenwood Cemetery, Elkton, as is Dr. Henry R. Bell, Jr., her grandson, the son of the late Henry R. and Kathie Street Bell

Glover and Betty Williams' wedding at the Cedar Hill Methodist Church, Cedar Hill, TN, on September 5, 1953

Joe and Anita Mobley Gray, married July 12, 1953, in Birmingham, Alabama. From left: bride's parents, Mr. and Mrs. William Mobley, Anita, Joe, and mother of the groom, Mrs. Edna Gray

August 20, 1959, George and Betty Brown's wedding

Joy Bell and Robert Haley, Jr., Dec. 26, 1959 wedding. From left: Wallace and Marion Bell, Joan Bell Phillips, Joy Bell and Robert Haley Jr., Carolyn and Robert Leo Haley

Golden wedding anniversary of Thomas and Lou Robertson, December 31, 1975

John Bouldin driving newlyweds Julie and Henry Hamlet

Danny Lee and Wilda Harrison on their wedding day, July 2, 1971

Wedding picture of M.A. and Louella Escue Dorris, 1892

Wedding of Jim Anderson and Mary Beaufort Smith, Aug. 19, 1945

Aaron and Buhler Hall Gillum married September 11, 1943. Buhler rode the train to California to marry Aaron, who was stationed there awaiting orders to serve in the South Pacific during W.W.II. They were married in San Luis Obispo, California. After Aaron shipped out, Buhler returned by train to her home in Stewart County, Tennessee.

Jack and Mavis Ezell Gray, married June 5, 1946, at the home of the bride's parents, Benjamin and Fannie Ezell in Dover, Tennessee

Alice Miller Chesnut, 1898

Left: Katie Lassiter Ryals' wedding portrait

SOCIAL ACTIVITIES AND RECREATION

A buggy full of young girls

M. A. Dorris and hunting dogs, Sharon Grove, KY

Growing up in a small town has lots of advantages-fast friends, from left: S.D. (Booger) Chesnut, Bobby Williams, Junnie Allen, and Teddy Woodall

Bikers in the '40's, from left: Sheridan Cole, Bobby Williams, Junnie Allen, Larry Tribble, and Teddy Woodall

Four young ladies, from left: Betty Stahl, Tula Carter, Mary Agnes Smith and Olivia Harrell

Dunbar Cave, Clarksville, TN, on the weekend nights was the place to be - to dance, meet new partners, and socialize. Martha Dean Patterson dancing with her partner, John Stahl

Norma Adams Meriwether, first on left, Guthrie, KY

Three couples, 1940, from left: Margaret Patrick, Robert Lawson, Willis Camp, Dorothy Dickinson, Lelia Barker, Charles Nabb

Felix Bryan in the 1940's

From left: Charles E. Burge, Gretta Burge in car, Dillard Payne

From left: Margaret Patrick Lawson, Mildred Payne Adams, Sara Smith, Katherine Patterson Patrick, Lelia Barker Nabb, and Dorothy Dickinson Camp

Orville and Mary G. Finney in the mid 1960's on their Allensville farm

Left: Posing on the Allen's lawn in Trenton are from left: Martha Dean Patterson, Dorothy Vernon Latham, Rosamond Ware

Front, from left: Ann Jones, June Camp. Back, from left: Eloise Camp, Jane Reason, Marilyn Camp, on the steps of the Trenton Methodist Church. Church burned in 1958.

From left: Betty Jean Covington, Margie Haley, Ned Glover, Bobby McMurrey, Junior/Senior Banquet, 1953

Glenn Hughes gets ready for a ride as Marilyn Sue Frogue holds the reins to the pony.

Bob Payne, John Bouldin, and Bill Sadler getting ready for a parade

Young couple in buggy Bryant Taylor and Mary Payne

Marilyn Frogue watches as son, Justin, tries his skill at riding the calf.

Southern Belle, Mary Dudley McClendon, poses for the camera

Dancing to the big bands that appeared at historic Dunbar Cave, Clarksville, TN, are S. D. (Booger) Chesnut and Anne Jones

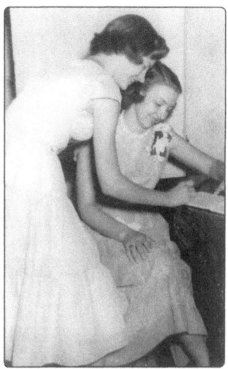

Kathleen Chastain Killebrew, left, and sister, Sarah Chastain Penick, 1956

Junnie Allen of Trenton shows acrobatic skills by standing effortlessly on fireplug.

Betty Stahl and Bobby Gene Allen, 1946

Second largest tree in Kentucky, located off Hwy. 104 near Trenton. Girls, from left: Rebecca Wieck, Sarah Lewis, Katie Lewis and Mary Wieck

Dorothy Miller and Tarleton Averitt receiving ribbons

R. T. (Tarleton) Averitt receiving honors with "Sons Naughty Lady"

Tarleton Averitt receiving honors with his Tennessee Walking Horse, "Miss Mary Go," in 1950

Tarleton Averitt receiving honors on "Miss Mary Go"

Nellie Ruth Camp on her pony, "Dixie"

Jockey : Theo Dickinson, Trenton, KY, Trainer: G. C. White - Taken at Tanforan, San Bruno, California-Owner-Rose Dale Stables

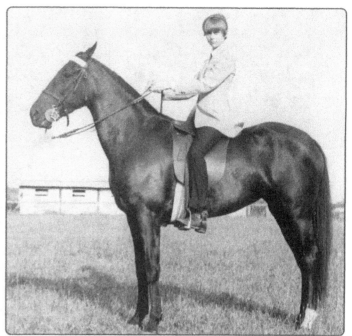

From left: Robert Seay, Leslie Seay, Thedo Seay, at Mericourt Park in Clarksville, Tennessee, 1962

Debbie Seay on her pleasure horse

Philathea Class at Trenton Baptist Church, General Jackson Cruise, from left: John and Sarah Bouldin, Clyde and Shirley Woods, Basil and Joann Beckelhimer, Robert and Peggy Glover, S. B. and Alma Carter, Ed and Nelle Brookshire, Dick and Emily Dickinson, and Dick and Sylvia Sadler

Sarah Averitt and Bobby Dickinson, 1959

Bernadene and Leren Gorrell at their home near Claymour

Georgia and Dorothy Watts, 1943, daughters of Mr. and Mrs. Frank P. Watts

Dressed in their finest waiting for the train to come by, in Trenton

Our gang in Trenton shooting marbles, from left: Dick Dickinson, Sam Binnaugh, Teddy Woodall, and Billy Moss

From right: Ray Baucum, S. D. (Booger) Chesnut, and Sheridan Cole clowning for the camera with their upper classman, Larry Tribble

Theo Dickinson, jockey, May 24, 1938

Dorothy Payne entertaining at her Trenton home.

Todd Central Students, 1967

Teen Town at Milliken Community House- Darnell Foster, Bill Weathers, Sue Penick, Nancy Cloud, Martha Penick, Sandra Smith, Mike Flack, 1965

Lucy F. Chastain and friend, Freida Cohoon, in Branson, Missouri. Lucy celebrated her 85th birthday on this trip.

Patricia Seay in her first competition with her Tennessee Walking Horse, "Justice Souvenir," in Columbia, TN in 1973

Hay baling in 1970

SESQUICENTENNIAL 1971

SESQUICENTENNIAL CELEBRATION 1971

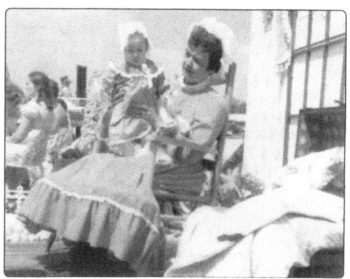

Margaret Ann Dill
Sesquicentennial Celebration,
1971

Joe Edwards, Keystone Cop,
2nd Kangaroo Court, April 10,
1971

"Snookie" Crouch and Jill Brown Sholar

Gracious Ladies of Sharon Grove, May 01, 1971, from left: Eula Wright, Mother of Paul J. and Hubert (Jr.) Wright, Geneva Spencer, mother of Sue Brown, Matilda Harris (retired Sharon Grove Postmaster) standing by her car decorated for the Sesquicentennial Parade in Elkton, KY. She is the mother of Bill Harris, Marjoria Munger, Pauline Routte and Louise Szalay.

Sesquicentennial Celebration, 1971, from left: Oscar Lewis Morhead, James Hightower, Joe Edwards, Darryl Edwards

Sesquicentennial Celebration, 1971

Sesquicentennial Celebration, 1971

Sesquicentennial Celebration, 1971. State's First RFD, Allensville, KY. From left: Richard B. Young, Post Master; Billy Penick, RFD carrier; Charles Breakfield and Eva Page, office staff

Mule Power - John Hunt of Bumpaw, KY with his mule drawn wagon and a passenger lined up to pull Sharon Grove's float in the Sesquicentennial Celebration, April 25-May 01, 1971. The float contained the Sesqui Belles (Froghoppers), from Sharon Grove Chapter.

Agriculture Day, Todd Co Sesquicentennial, 1971

Geneva Spencer, April 1971 in one of her homemade outfits, going to a tea held during the Todd County Sesquicentennial. Celebration was held from April 25-May 01, 1971. Geneva was in the Sharon Grove Chaper of the Sesquicentennial Belles.

SPECIAL EVENTS

John Bouldin and young friends in the Hopkinsville Parade

Fall Festival Parade, Elkton, KY

John Bouldin gets the covered wagon ready for parade route

John Bouldin ready for parade

Tony Seay hauls precious cargo, Kelly, Kyle, Kylene Penick and Lori Thompson in the Adams, Tennessee parade

John Bouldin, Adams, TN, parade

Louis Gossett, Jr. of This Man Stands Alone

Doris (Martin) Kelly with actor Clu Gulager of This Man Stands Alone

Mel Tillis and Margaret Lawson

1981 Miss Confederacy, Shelley Cole, with father, Sheridan Cole

Blanche and Tarleton Averitt at the Tennessee Walking Horse Celebration, Box Seat E-58

Trenton High School Junior-Senior Banquet, 1953. From left: Sarah Averitt, Shirley Higgins, Jimmy Trevena, and Melvin Dickinson.

A picnic in the woods in the lake area. Katie Lassiter in the sailor dress and Hugh Garrot Ryals at the right

Robert Lawson dressed for womanless wedding in Trenton, KY

Local twirlers model sport outfits for a fashion show in the Trenton Gymnasium. From left: Denise Ware, Ginger Williams, Joann Dickinson, Ruth Lawson, Melanie Howell, Evelyn Gray

In the early sixties, students from Todd County High, Elkton, formed a variety talent group called The Antons. The Antons performed around the region at county fair talent shows. Their last performance was at the Tennessee State Miss America Pageant in Jackson. Dancers, from left: Regina Perry Ramsey, Jackie Boyd, Pricilla Carver Buchberg, Paula Young Gibbs, Anne Maynard Brandon and Myrtle Ann Brooks Mudge. Band members, standing from left: Morton Bell, Dr. A. G. Campbell, Bill Weathers and Darnell Foster. Seated, from left: Lizz Boyd, Ann Henderson Gardner, Lynn Markham Roe and Genie Everett

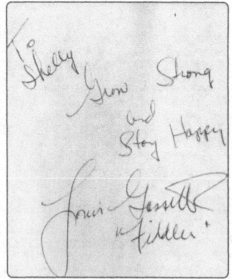

Portrait and autograph, of Lewis (Lou) Gossett, academy award winning actor, given to Shelley Cole during the filming of This Man Stands Alone *in Todd County, 1978*

Helen Martin, actress of This Man Stands Alone

Swimming in the DUCK POND, 1923, Dick Smith and family, Trenton, KY

ARMY DAY in Elkton, KY, April 6, 1942

Birthday party for Chris Cole, second from right. Guests: Mike Taylor, Kathy Williams, Joel Cole, Trenton Guinn, Ginger Williams, Melinda Guinn, Teddy Frazier, David Chesnut. Chris had his fifth birthday party and received a baby sister, Shelley, born on his birthday, Jan. 23, 1964.

Hog killing time, late 1930's. From left: Fred King, M. A. Dorris, Coy Dorris, Romie Gant

SCHOOLS, CLASSES, CLUBS

Elkton High School, 1939

1932-33 Juniors and Seniors in Mr. Gardners Chemistry Class at Elkton High School

Trenton High School shortly after the building was completed in 1920

Trenton School, 1940's

Trenton School P.T.A. officers, 1940's. From left: Mrs. Anna Chesnut, Mrs. Cora Woodall, Mrs. Selma Camp, Mrs. Elizabeth Ann Jones

Classmates-Friends: Patty Glover, Mary B. Camp, Mary Jane Peters, Billy Chesnut, Glover Williams, M. R. Crutchfield, Jr., Frank Cox, Cliff Camp, Jr., Pattie Lawson, Sarah Luttrull, John Crutchfield and Nellie Ruth Camp

Better English Club, Sharon Grove High School. First row, from left: Ewing Troutt, Gerald Wright, Wilbur Dorris, Bernice Porter. Second row: Lucy Cook, Eula Hadden, Willye Glenn, Beulah Tomerlin, Patie Wilkins, Anna Belle Dorris, Martha Turner, Nellie Borders. Third row: Eunice Lyon, Dura Lyan, Vela McBride, Thelma Gorrell, Fannye Gant, Edna Borders, Anna Belle Crowder, Ara Heltsley, Gladys Porter. This club was organizd by Professor R. A. Demunbrun at the beginning of the school year 1923-24.

Mrs. Vera Royster, Trenton School teacher, 1940's

Elkton High School 1st and 2nd grade class, 1937, teacher, Mrs. Davis. First row, from left: Tom Byrum, Charles Boyer, Houston Walton, H. K. Gann, J. L. Hollingsworth, June Byrum, Charles Kimbrough, James Howell, Gerald Reeves, unidentified. Second row, from left: Dorothy Ann Kimbrough, Patsy Draper, Paula Graves, Evelyn Walker, Annie Mae Patterson, Elizabeth Overby, Marie Petty Jean Bland, Gloria Olmstead, Betty Stahl. Third row, from left: Bobby Darke, James Stahl, Waldo Wolfe, Rudolph Patterson, Mrs. H. G. Davis, Edith Chastain, Louise Patterson, Geraldine Stahl. Fourth row, from left: Terry Finn, Evelyn Cowherd, Betty Ruth Dillary, Glen Latham, Kenneth East, Tommy Morgan, Ruby Pennycuff

Mrs. Lucy Pennington, Trenton teacher for many years, 1946

*School Days
Harlan Stratton, 1948-49*

*School Days
Elnora Blake, 1934*

*School Days
Rowena Blake, 1934*

*Senior picture of Mary
Chastain Cohoon from
Elkton High School, 1948*

*Clyde Wallace
Dickinson, "Sop"*

*From left: Isabelle Adams Glascock, Lelia (Sis) Barker Nabb, Isabel
Crutchfield (known as Lasses), and Ted (Pete Chesnut's dog). Taken
on the Trenton school house steps, first day of school, 1926*

*Bottom, from left: Polly Ann Maynard Allen, Mildred Carr, Dorothy
Sue Lawson Sweeney, Dorcas Bell, Ruth Edwards Willis, Carolyn
Payne Ryals. Back row, from left: Carol McAllen, Dorothy Bell
Orr, Margarite Dickinson Hyams, Dorothy Nabb, Agnes May Glover*

*Sharon Grove Elementary, circa 1900, teacher, Jim Malone. Back
row, extreme left: T. W. Hall. Back row, extreme right: Mrs. T. W. Hall*

Sharon Grove School, 1933; Teacher Fred Wilkins

Left: Nannie Williams Fortson with grandson, Michael Robert Chastain, on the event of her MA degree from Western Kentucky Teachers' College in June 1948.

Middle: Nannie W. Fortson on her porch steps in Guthrie, KY, in August 1966

Right: Mattie Sanders, Guthrie teacher, with student

High School students at front entrance of Trenton High School in 1941

Graduating Class, Elkton High School, 1937

Mattie Sanders, teacher, with her first grade students at Guthrie Elementary in 1963

Construction of the Trenton School Gymnasium in cooperation with Works Progress Administration (WPA) in Kentucky, 1936

Fulcher's School, above and right, was a one-room schoolhouse located at the intersection of what is now Fulchers School Rd. and Maton Rd. Fulcher's photographs were taken about 1940 and include all students enrolled at that time. Miss Francis Coleman was the teacher, back row, left, in the photo above.

From left: Jim Dickinson, Clyde Wallace Dickinson, Dorothy Bell Orr, Dorothy Sue Lawson Sweeney, Robert Taylor, Charles Glascock, Carol McElwain Allen and (behind) Martha Elizabeth Adams Luttrull

Shannon Taylor and Jim Jobe in kindergarten

From left: Mattie Sanders and Marie Lennon, Teachers Gene Everett, Pennyrile REA Representative Tony Winders, 3rd place winner, Courier-Journal and Louisville Times Poster Contest; Nancy Johnson, 2nd place winner, Courier-Journal and Louisville Times Essay Contest; W.O. Watts, Jr., Todd Co. Conservation District Supervisor; Larry Tribble, Guthrie Elementary Principal

From left: unidentified, Karen and Billy Hogan on the play ground of Trenton School

Front row, from left: Doug Dossett, Raymond Latham, Jr., unidentified, Jame Brumfield (Combs), Mary Ewing (Sweeney), Betty Shanklin Simpkins, Virginia Hill, Ruth Brumfield Shanklin. Back row, from left: unidentified, James Dossett, Tom Shanklin, Teacher, Willie Sue Simons. 1947

Faculty Members at Trenton Independent School, 1946. Front, from left: Miss Eileen Kirkland and Miss Juanita McDougal (Mrs. Lewis Dickinson). Back, from left: Will Logan, superintendent and teacher, and Jimmy Jones, principal, coach and teacher

Right: Front row, from left: Terry Moore Latham, Glendolyn Brumfield (Alder), Tommy Dossett, Robert Jones, unidentified, Betty Hill (Noel), Betty Brumfield Latham. Back row, from left: unidentified, unidentified, William Ewing, Eula Ewing Monroe. Back right: Teacher, Willie Sue Simons

Mr. Joe Waller, Trenton School custodian, 1940's

Mrs. Judith Waller, teacher, at the front entrance of Trenton High School

Nannie Williams Fortson taken at the Guthrie School in 1950

Left: Mr. Will G. Logan, superintendant of Trenton Independant School

Classmates at Trenton High School, from left: Margie Haley, Joan Camp, Elizabeth Newcomb, Sarah Seay, unidentified, unidentified, Billy Watts, Glenda Green, unidentified, Linda Glover

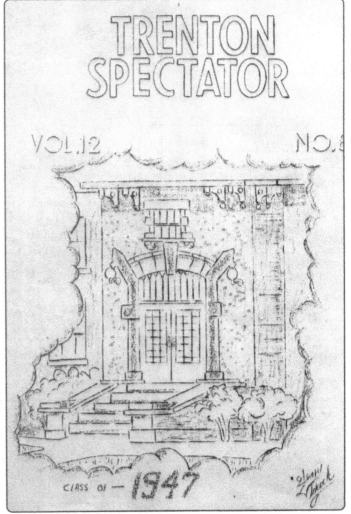

Trenton High School monthly publication, Trenton Spectator, cover illustrating the entrance to the school building in 1947

Mt. Sharon School, 1893. Back row, left: Mrs. A. E. Gant holding young son, Romie Gant

Guthrie Graded Schools, A. J. Haun, Principal, 1907-08, Guthrie, Ky

Guthrie Graded School, 1910

Opening day at Trenton Independent School, 1922. Note some students sitting and kneeling in the upstairs windows

4-H Club, circa 1940

Glee Club at Trenton High School, school year 1952-53

Senior High Forensics Club, Trenton, 1950

John Locke School, Elkton, KY, Commercial Dept. Class, 1919-1920

Guthrie School, 1937, third and fourth grades

June 2, 1915, Miss Annie Nold Wells, school teacher, seated at the side entrance to the old Elkton Public School building. Miss Wells served for many years as Circuit Court Clerk in Todd County.

Trenton School, 5th Grade, 1958. Top row from left: Sandra Smith, Billie Payne Ryals, David Camp, J. W. Westerman, Nancy Cloud, Patsy Arnett. Second row from left: Billy Delozier, Mike Flack, Gayle Sisk, Rodney Seay, Bill Campbell, Sue Penick. Bottom row from left: Katherine Evans, teacher Martha Penick, Bruce Moore, Richard Watts, Martha Jo Rutledge, Ross Dickinson, Franklin Williams

Year 1921-22. First: Elizabeth Kimbrough, Maude L. Moody, Virginia Evans, Ed Bryan, Howard Morgan, James Newton, Raymon Martin, Lasie Stahl, Mr. Edmiston, Mr. Parks, Mary Taylor, Dorothy Nelson, Margaret Moody, Mary Warren, Elizabeth Lannom, Elizabeth Jordan, Louise Bryan, Oliver Boone, Pauline Wyman. Second: Thelma Broaders, Ruby Dodson, Nannie Tyler, Willie Hampton, Annie Ried Greenfield, Felix Bryan, Tipp Allensworth, Warren Slack, Hulin Gower, Thomas Allensworth, Archie Scott, George Boswell, Whayne Guinn. Third: Lucile Hines, Hazel Boone, Mary Gray, Sue Belle Wyate, Murry Slack, Bobby Murry, W. E. Rogers, Helen Tyler, Ruby Hampton, Helen Sevann, Sottie Bradley, Dorsie Vaughn

Trenton School Class, 1923, 1st and 2nd grades. Picture taken third year after building the new school.
Bottom row, from left: Sue Clark, Mary Edloe Mimms, Howard Dickinson, Marshal House, Allen
Northington. Second row, from left: Billy Anderson, Louise Self, Mary Elizabeth Clark, ?, Roy Young, ?.
Third row, from left: Ruth Edwards, ? Northington, Mildred Carr, Marquerite Dickinson, unidentified,
Polly Ann Maynard, unidentified, Becky Maynard. Fourth row, from left: Louis Sadler, Allen Murphy,
William (Frog) Nabb, Garrott Ryals, Edward Lee (Blue Wing) Payne, George Dickinson, Garth Camp,
Billy Ryals. On left side, bottom, Phil Dickinson, Clarence Sadler. Top left: Mimms Dickinson. Top right:
Boots Evans. Bottom right: Katherine Hatcher

Bottom row, from left: Clyde Wallace Dickinson, James Barker, Jim Dickinson, Charles Glascock.
Second row, from left: Carol McElwain Allen, Edgar Hutchinson, Dorothy Sue Lawson Sweeney,
Everett Wilson, Dorothy Bell Orr, James Owen Anderson, Martha Elizabeth Adams Luttrull

John Locke School, Elkton, KY, founded in 1892 by Louisville Conference M. E. Church South

Trenton School, second grade; teacher: Mrs. Flora Mae Thompson. Front row, from left: Martha Moore, Larry Frederick, Judy Anderson, Genesue Seay, Mary Ruth Scott, Sandra Patrick, Ronnie Smith. Back row, from left: Mike Fish, Joan Cox, Brock Simmons, Paul Arnett, Sharon Patterson, Mike Weatherford, Dorothy Jean Scott.

Kirkmansville High School, mid 1930's

Kirkmansville High School, mid 1930's

Trenton High School - First row, from left: Elizabeth Killebrew, Jean Tribble, Miss Juanita Dickinson, teacher, Betty Stahl, Ruth Campbell, Mary Agnes Smith. Second row, from left: Austin Leavell, Edith Hamlet, Waller Dickinson, Bobby Allen

Guthrie Elementary School, fifth grade, 1969-70 school year. First year teacher, Mrs. Lelia Cole

Todd Co. School System's end-of-year "Best Students' Day," 1947

Katherine Menees' 2nd grade class, 1947, Guthrie Elementary

Class picture in 1927-28. Teacher, Claude Hightower, is at right front. Mr. Hightower later became the superintendant of Todd County Schools.

First grade class, Guthrie Elementary. Mattie Sanders, teacher. 1963

Todd County Board of Education, 1957. Seated: Oscar Sullivan, left, and James Latham. Standing, from left: Boss Hampton, Wilbur Cole, Jimmy Weathers, Wilbur Gregory, Warren Claytor.

School group on the front of Trenton School steps

High school students on the steps of the Trenton Gymnasium, 1941

Allensville School construction, Aug. 24, 1936-Aug 27, 1937

Left: Sammy Porter, Guthrie, KY

Right: New gymnasium in Trenton almost completed by the Works Progress Administration in 1936

Best friends: Shirley Higgins, seated, and Sarah Averitt

Sarah Averitt at Trenton School, 1948

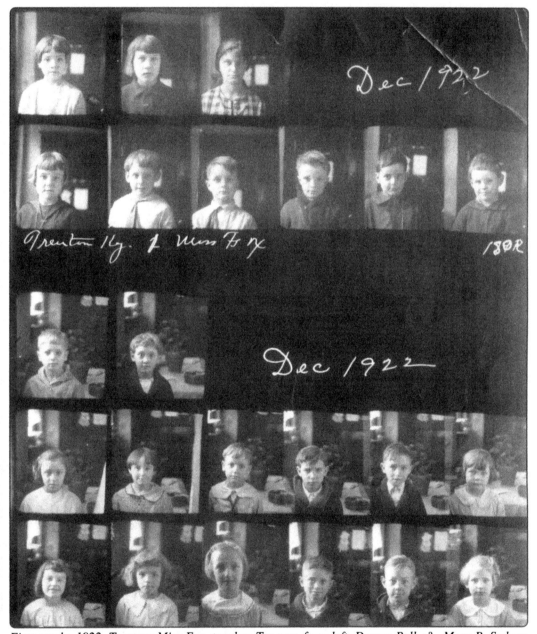

First grade, 1922, Trenton; Miss Fox, teacher. Top row, from left: Dorcas Bell, ? , Mary B. Sydnor. Second row, from left: Carolyn Payne, Herbert Anderson, Jim Gower Glascock, Charles Lewis Waller, A. Garth House, Allen Northing. Third row, from left: Will Cobb, Theo Dickinson. Fourth row, from left: Hazel Keeney, Dorothy Nabb Warfield Smith, Mimms Dickinson, "Boots" Evans, Ruth Edwards. Bottom row, from left: Mildred Carr, ?, Marguerite Dickinson, Donald Murphy, ? , Katherine Hatcher

SCHOOL ACTIVITIES

Freshman Class, Guthrie High School, 6 November 1924. Those numbered: 1. Paul Northington, 2. Bobby McMurry, 3. Whayne Quin, 4. Jennie Snadon, 5. Thomas Warren, 6. William Edmiston, Principal, 7. Billy Covington, 8. Willie Hampton, 9. J. P. Morgan, 10. Louise Bryan, 11.Granville Frey, 12. Carolyn Moody, 13. Lorene Rogers, 14. Dorothy Nelson, 15. Tipp Allensworth.

Guests at the Tom Thumb Wedding on April 12, 1940, Trenton High School, documented by Mrs. Selma Camp. Listed, from left, by name, age and character portrayed: June Summers Camp, age 3, as Little Lord Fauntleroy; Marilyn Sue Camp, age 8, as mother of the bride; Anna Cox, age 9, as the grandmother; Linda Glover, age 5, as Ann Shirley (movie star); Larry Tribble, age 7, as Mortimer Snerd (an Edgar Bergin dummy); James Robert Smith, age 8, as Robert Taylor (movie star); Hatcher Smith, age 8, as president Franklin D. Roosevelt; Barbara Camp, age 8, as First Lady Eleanor Roosevelt; Tula Carter, age 10, as the Dutchess of Windsor; Jack Garth (Bob Payne's half-brother), age 7, as the Duke of Windsor; Edward Camp, age 10, as Lord Chamberlain; Clyde F. Chesnut, age 8, as Rhett Butler; Sarah Booher (Methodist preacher's daughter), age 10, as Scarlett O'Hara; Robin Williams, age 9, as Paul Sullivan (news columnist); Polly M. Allen, age 8, as Emily Post; Sarah K. Payne, age 8, as Mrs. Rober Taylor; Freddie Schuerman, age 8, as Charlie McCarthy (an Edgar Bergin dummy); Anne Bransford, age 5, as Confucius; Martha Cox, age 8, as Dorothy Thompson (news columnist); Martha Dean Patterson, age 8, as Queen Mary; Sue Carolyn Payne, age 8, as Shirley Temple; Irene Luttrell, age 9, as the mother of the groom; Cindy Crutchfield, age 9, as Ann Southern (movie star); Jimmie Jones, age 7, as Kay Kyser (big band "Kay Kyser & His Musical Knights"); Marjorie Ann Smith, age 8, as Ginnie Sims (who sang with Kay Kyser's orchestra).

Serving and looking at the camera, Geneva Stokes. In lunch line, Sarah Seay, Linda Glover, Clyde Woods and Teddy Woodall

Waiting patiently for lunch in the old Trenton High School cafeteria

Guthrie High School Graduation, 1945. Norma Adams Meriwether, last female on the right

Chasing butterflies. Lucy F. Chastain with her first graders after a unit on butterflies

Senior Class Play, 1955, from left: Lelia Chastain, Shirley Higgins, Sarah Averitt, Morris Mullins, Shirley Simmons and Marvin Jones

Trenton School Senior Play

Tom Thumb Wedding at Trenton Independent School, 1941, from left: Ann Jones, Melvin Dickinson, Betty Jean Covington, Booger Chesnut, Ann Flack, ? Bennett, Peg Crutchfield, Jean Chesnut, Rosamond Ware, Talles Allen Jr., Henry Bell, the minister, Richard Dickinson, Billy Watts, Dorothy Vernon Latham, Bob Crutchfield, Polly Maynard, Ed Denny Crouch, Mary Dickinson, Teddy Woodall.

Trenton Halloween Carnival King/Queen: Paul Kerr and Joanne Lawson, 1st grade

Trenton Halloween Carnival King/Queen: Joanne Lawson and Paul Kerr, 8th grade, 1965

Judy Anderson Donnelly plays the fortune teller at the Todd County Schools' Fair

Amy Roberts and others standing in line with Trenton Elementary trip to the 1982 World's Fair in Knoxville, TN

School buddies, from left; Bottom: Wilson Claytor, James Rogers Turner. Middle: Allen Dickinson, Jerry Cobb, Bobby Taylor, Dan Smith. Back: Grant Dickinson, Bobby Dickinson, Barry Cole, 1950

Trenton Elementary School 8th grade weekend class trip to the Biltmore in North Carolina, 1975

Trentonian Yearbook Staff, 1952. Seated, from left: Margie Davis, Lorraine Gilliam, Joyce Leavell, Dick Dickinson, Sarah Seay, Jimmy Jones, Joan Camp, Joyce Chester. Standing, from left: Dan Riggins, Clyde Woods, Glenda Green, Nello Stokes, Earl Cornell, Mary Dickinson, Jimmy Murrey, Rosamond Ware, Phil Waggoner, Mary D. McClendon, Dorothy Vernon Latham, Jean Chesnut, Elizabeth Newcomb, Ed Denny Crouch, Billy Watts, Bob Crutchfield, Linda Glover, Boyd Joiner

Mr. Claude and "Miss" Virginia Hightower, Junior-Senior Banquet, May 1957

SCHOOL SPORTS

Trenton Basketball Team, 1946. First row, from left: Billy Chesnut, Glover Williams, Bobby Allen. Second row, from left: Cliff Camp, Frank Cox, Mr. James H. Jones, coach.

Guthrie High School Basketball Team, 1912-13. From left: Flood, McClure, Linebaugh, Greenfield, Rosson, Prof. Clarpool

Guthrie High School Football Team, 1907-08. Front row: William McMurry, Mack Linebaugh, Aubrey Flood, Mose Brenner, Dorrel Carter, Irvin Linebaugh, George McCrow; Second row: Pete Baler. Third row: Marshall Greenfield, Jack Allen, Lyman Moulton, Chas Hooper. Back: Prof. A. J. Hann

Guthrie High School, 1910. First row, from left: Pete Baler, Wm McMurray, Marshall Greenfield, Mack Linebaugh, Jim Dority, Hugh Coke, Lyman Moulton, Mel McMurray, Willie Small. Second row: Louis Rosson. Third row: Principal C. H. Gifford, Howard Rosson Edgar Evans, Luther Coke. Front: Cyrus Greenfield

Kirkmansville High School Basketball Team, 1932

Cheerleaders, from left: Jane Reasons, Sarah Payne, Tula Carter, Ann Dickinson, and Eloise Camp, 1946

Allensville Baseball Team

Cheerleaders, from left: Jeanie Wheeler, Betty Tatum, Patsy Howell, Karen Hogan and Mamie Dickinson

Guthrie High School Team, 1930

Kentucky State Basketball Tournament, Louisville, Kentucky, 1957, Elkton Elks. Team members, from left: Harold Rose, Harold W. Snead, Bobby Stokes, John Camp, James E. Stokes, and Bobby Collins

Trenton Elementary Girls' Basketball Team

Trenton Elementary Cheerleaders, from left: Georgie Sumpter, Kim Glenn, Angela Lewis, Yvonne Green, Lynn Wilkins. Top: Pattie Kaye McCuiston

Trenton Dragons, 1957-58, from left: Billy Overton, William Empson, Billy Ray Turner, unidentified, Jerry Cobb, Jack Roberts, and Wilson Claytor. "We looked ragged, but we won a lot of games."

Elkton High School, 1953-54 Cheerleaders. From left: Barbara Hurt, Sissy Camp, Roma Smith, Joy Bell, Gayle Wilson

Elkton High School Football Team, 1941

Standing: Coach-Billy Wayne Covington. From left: Billy Joe Glenn, Walter Thomas, Jesse Owen Robertson, Johnny Payne, James Roy Belcher, Bobby Frey, Wally Williams, Bill Longhurst Jr., Owen Banton

HOMES

The Pepper Place in Allensville was built in 1864 by local merchant E. A. Yost. In 1880, Mr. Yost sold the home to Dr. Isaac Walton as a residence and medical office. The home and 100 acres were purchased in 1895 by Mr. and Mrs. Philip Hirshfeld as a wedding present for their daughter, Mrs. Thomas Pepper. Photo circa 1895. From left: Ida Pepper, unknown woman, Thomas Pepper, Philip Hirshfeld, unknown man, and Mrs. Hirshfeld. The Kentucky Heritage Council has designated The Pepper Place a Kentucky Landmark.

The home of Felix E. Bryan burned to the ground in the 1990's. Built before the Civil War

The Robert (Bob) and Dorothy Payne home in Trenton, KY

Old Burge Home in Trenton. Site of new home of Charlie Payne

Home of Ann S. Chesnut, Trenton

Burge Homeplace, Trenton, KY

Snadon home located on Highway 79 facing Snardon Mill Road. The land originally belonged to the first George Snadon. The original home burned, and this one was built on the foundation of the first house. It was the home of John Franklin Snadon and his wife Susan Frances Weatherford. About 1918, it was occupied by Frank Dabney Snadon, grandson of John and Susan, and his wife Jennie Lawrence, along with their daughter Jennie Snadon.

Idlewild, the Banks' Home, on U.S. 41 in Trenton, KY. Circa 1892. Pictured are Georgianna (Joy) Sebree Banks (1855-1928) and two of her five daughters. She was married at Idlewild to Strother Jones Banks (1841-1927) in 1879. Current owners Dr. and Mrs. Robert Haley

Residence of George Snadon, located north of the Mimms home on the opposite side of the street. The home burned.

Meriville, home of the Meriwether family. Built in 1809, by Dr. Charles Meriwether, Guthrie, KY

Country home of William Clay and Selma Camp. Built in 1884 by Henry Clay White. The brick were burned on the site.

Breezewood, circa 1852. Original section circa 1839. Built by Dabney Smith. Current owners, Gary and Judy Anderson Donnelly. Judy is a direct descendant of Dabney Smith.

Unidentified lady posing on the Castle porch in Guthrie, KY, 1930

Millen Home - site of the most horrible tragedy in all Todd's history. Frank Millen, a prominent young farmer, killed his father, Charlie Millen, his mother, Bettie, his brother, Elmo, and Elmo's wife, Annie Howell Millen, a bride of three months, and then killed himself. May 9, 1917

One of Trenton's Historic Old Country Homes. Pioneer settler, Reuben Bradley, selected this spot to settle on in 1830. Around 1850, he built this home with three large rooms and hall on the first floor and two bedrooms on the second floor. The kitchen was detached from the main house with a 'dogtrot' connecting it to the main house. A large basement across the entire front was a part of the original building. Reuben Bradley's daughter, Eliza, married James S. Gillis. They sold the farm to G. A. LePrade, who in turn sold the farm on November 15, 1873, to R. M. Hogan. At his death, his son Russell Hogan became the owner. In the early 1900's, the present porch was added across the front and the small window panes gave way to the present type. A study of the picture displayed here today shows the home before these changes took place. Russell Hogan's son, Richard Hogan, repeated the pattern established by his father and grandfather. He lived in the home place from 1949 until his death in 1960. With each generation the Hogan home was the scene of many happy reunions and community social functions.

R. T. (Tarleton) Averitt's home, 1947

Farm home of Mr. and Mrs. Ray Miller from 1939-1977. Located on Old Allensville Rd. Picture made in the 1940's

Harrison Home Place on Collier Springs Road

CHURCHES

The Kathleen Payne Class of the Trenton Baptist Church, May 9, 1937

Congregation of the Trenton Methodist Church on the front steps in 1912. Baby in the center back being held by her father is Belle Maynard, who later married Parker Bell

Ladies' Class at the Trenton Baptist Church. Front row, from left: Opal Vinson, Lucy Camp, Martha Ware, Gertrude Garth, Mary Arvin, Mallie Taylor, Selma Camp. Second row, from left: Cora Woodall, Josephine Camp, Melissa Arvin, Elsie Northern, Lillian Thompson, Maude Roberts. Third row, from left: Nan Radford, Virginia Garth, Blanche Averitt, Mabel Joiner. Back row, from left: Virginia Camp, Arbee Allen, Gladys Chesnut

Trinity Church organized September 18, 1967 (Old Church House), located on 181 Greenville Rd.

Trinity General Baptist Church joined Long Creek Association October 9, 1981. (New Church House Building) Present Pastor: Rev. Autry Moore

Pleasant Hill United Methodist Church, destroyed by fire, Jan. 17, 1999

Ground breaking for the new church

New Pleasant Hill U. M. Church

Aerial view of Bells Chapel Church, 1970

Baptism in the creek; Sept, 07, 1975, Bro. Weldon Epley baptizing Bobby Joe Brown in Antioch Creek after he joined Sharon Grove Baptist Church. Bobby lived next door to the church.

Trenton Methodist Church Choir, Feb. 1958

Trenton Baptist Church

First Communion Class. Sts. Mary and James Church, 1961. From left: Joe Park, Gerry Covington and Mary Elizabeth Sanders

Isabelle Glascock, far left, with local children as Mrs. Luna Harris, far right, gives the old church bell (in frame) back to the church after new church was built with a bell tower.

100 Year Celebration of the Claymour Camp Meeting-1904-2003. The effects of Kentucky's Great Revival of 1800 arrived late in Claymour. Religious fervor came to Claymour in 1904. A group who had been motivated by religious zeal established the Claymour Camp Meeting. A secluded spot in the woods along the curve of Whippoorwill Creek was given to the Camp Meeting Association by F. S. Heltsley. The Association held its' first annual two-week meeting under a brush arbor. For the second meeting in 1905, a tabernacle was erected. Here and there around the structure were smaller buildings, in which those who lived far away could camp and attend the services. Since its' birth, the Camp Meeting has continued its' interdenominational sessions. It remains strong, popular and influential and its' future seems assured. From Mr. John C. Wright. Issues of the Todd County Standard

Collier Spring's Church was built with the purpose of being a spititual lighthouse in the community, and it still gracefully stands after 90 years as a testimony to all who enter its doors

Collier Spring's General Baptist Church, original church

Mt. Zion Baptist Church

Mt. Zion was adopted by the Arm of Bethel Church located at Salubria Springs, near Pembroke, in 1820. Mt. Zion became an independent chuch in 1824. The church was located on the Bluff of

West Fork Creek, a short distance from Lon Wrights', south of Trenton. This was a one room log building. Elder Isaiah Boone, brother of Daniel Boone, conducted services. In 1824, he became the first pastor. Elder Thomas Watts was the first minister to be ordained at Mt. Zion, July 1830.

Mt. Zion later built a meeting place deeded by Mr. McDougle on

Mt. Zion Baptist Church, Trenton

Clarksville Pike. This was a log building, also opposite the present church building. It was also used as a school.

In 1860, plans were made for a new building. On April 27, 1861, they reported they contracted for a new building for $2,400.00. Due to the Civil War, they later contracted for $5,150.00 on June 25, 1867. The old church sold for $250.00.

Later, Sunday School rooms and a fellowship room were added to the rear of the church. A vestibule was added to the front and also a steeple.

Mt. Zion at first belonged to the Red River Association but withdrew. A new association was formed in October 28, 1825, and was called Bethel, which consisted ot the following churches: Red River, Spring Creek, Drakes Pond, Mr. Gilead, Bethel, Little West Fork, Hoptown, then called New Providence and Pleasant Grove. The three churches received later were Elkton, Lebanon, and Mt. Zion.

Mrs. Agnes Mae Jones, Mt. Zion Historian

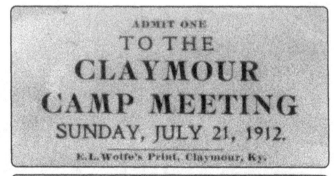

Northwest street scene in Trenton, showing the rock Methodist Church, Dr. Woodall's office, Hurst's Drug Store, Trenton Post Office, Dr. Gower's home, and the J. B. Williams' building. Methodist Church burned in 1958.

Claymour Camp Meeting Tickets, 1912-1913, found in a treasure box belonging to Dorothy Jean Knight's mother

Mt. Tabor Baptist Church Promotion of High Sunday School attendance of 175. Pastor J. R. Craig eats lunch on roof top as congregation looks on, April 7, 1984.

Mt. Sharon United Methodist Church

Guthrie United Methodist Church

Martha Elizabeth Adams Luttrull on the front steps to the Trenton Methodist Church

Bottom row, from left: Lucian Camp, Lewis Rutledge, Warren Claytor. Middle row, from left: Dr. J. C. Woodall, Paul Sisk, Bob Payne, James Adams, Bert Joiner. Top row, from left: Tommy Vinson, Willis Camp, R. T. Averitt, Bro. Earl Northern

AGRICULTURE

Sawmill at Pea Ridge

Workers in the Pea Ridge Community

Rufus Dickerson, left, and Robert Lawson, by the steam engine that was used to steam tobacco plant beds. The machine belonged to the Watts' family. After the steam engine was put to rest, tobacco plant beds were made by using cans of gas under a plastic canvas and later seeds were sowed and a canvas was put on top of the plant bed.

Robert Lawson on tractor with his father, Jim Lawson, on top of the threshing machine. Wheat was cut with a binder and tied, then dumped on the ground. Men would pick up the bundles and put them in shocks. When the thresher moved into the field, the shocks were loaded on a wagon and carried to the thresher and the machine would separate the grain from the straw.

Robert Lawson with a bull rake carrying hay to the stable to be carried up in the stable loft. A fork would be let down from the loft and wrapped around the hay and a horse at the back of the stable would pull the hay up and dump it in the loft. Margaret Lawson still has the bull rake used during the 1940's.

Uncle John Ware was part Indian and part Negro. He lived to be over 100 years old. He dug May apples and ginseng over the country to sell.

Joe Neale Fox, 1962

Robert (left) and Joe Lawson pulling a binder. This was used to cut and tie wheat.

Wheat harvest on the John Simpson farm on Davis Mill Road near Elkton.

Henderson Patrick cutting tobacco next to the Patrick home.

Tobacco barn located on the Ray Miller farm, when purchased in 1939. Still standing in 2003

Grainery on the Ray Miller farm. Built in the early forties

Cattle barn on Ray Miller farm. Built in the 1940's

Ray Miller standing in field of his first tobacco crop in 1916

Farmer's Hampshire Buck Sheep with Ewing E. Farmer in 1940

Daily Chore - Louella Dorris, wife of M. A. Dorris

Cotton picking in Trenton, KY. Man in center is Dab Smith.

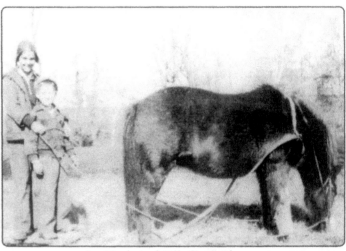

Joe Neale and Billy Fox with pony

Edwom C. and Ewing E. Farmer cutting dark tobacco in 1940

James E., Edwin C., and Ewing E. Farmer, and hired man, 1940, at Edwin's farm on Cemetery Rd. in Trenton

Todd County Conservation District Demonstration 1972. Farmers on tour to observe no till planted corn. Front row, from left: UK Extension Agent, Lewis Dickinson, Marvin Davidson, Frank Cox, Bucky Teeter, Joe Neale Fox, Mr. Britt, Bus Driver, Earl Wiles, Billy Fox, Eugene Keeton, Eston Glover. Back row, from left: Karl Harper, Mr. Henderson, George Street Boone, unidentified, unidentified, unidentified, Jim Ramey, Demos Andrews, Guy Keeton, Malcolm Sadler, William Buckley, Mr. Miller, Doug Henshaw, Allen Franks, Wallace White, David Crouch, Don Clampett, Floyd Smith, Henry Hampton, E. T. West, Joe M. Gill, and Chester Driskill

Henry Brown Stinson, 1888-1979, lived in Todd County all his life. He was known for his split hickory tobacco sticks, which he sold to local farmers. Henry used a froe that had originally belonged to his wife's grandmother.

Billy and Shirley Wyatt, Barton's children

Undertaking establishment of M. V. Lyon, Sharon Grove, KY. M. V. Lyon was often assisted by son in law, A. E. Gant, and grandson, Romie Gant. Picture taken 1962

Good corn crop in 1954

Howard Martin shown with his Martin Row Cleaner invention for no-till planting. This photo appeared in the Kentucky Prairie Farmer's February 5, 1991 edition.

Steam engine and threshing machine delivered to B. F. Groves, Sr., Train Depot, Central City, Ky. Pictured B. F. Groves, Jr., Mike Groves, B. F. Groves, Sr., Lear, Horace Groves

4-H Boys, from left: Dudley Garth, Richard White, Frank Dillard Payne, Jake Short, and county agent, D. H. Gooding, Memphis Fairgrounds, 1928

"Granny" Chastain feeding her chickens, early 1940's.

Jerome Bell feeding his chickens in Guthrie, KY

Tarleton Averitt with his Border collies

R. T. Averitt with his great grandson, Chris, his sheep, and Border collies

From left: Hayward Bell, ? Epley, Coy Edmonds, Norman Fox, Sr., Ned Bell driving the tractor, and in the rear, Billy Fox, 1943

John Bouldin with "Clay Gray"

Jasper Stratton in his turkey barn in Elkton, 1950

Fox farm workers in the early 1940's

Mike and Bobby Joe Brown standing by giant sunflower in their parents' (Joe and Sue) garden in Sharon Grove, July 21, 1969

Roland Rust, 1948

Carl Templeman plowing tobacco

Roland Rust plowing in 1945

From left: Carl, Delinda and Phil Templeman

TRANSPORTATION

Smith Chastain in Aunt Ella and Uncle Tom Anderson's front yard in 1945

Alma Lear Powell, Mayne Lear Sweeney, and William Lear, 1930

Margaret Meriwether on the right

Carl Templeman in front of car, 1930

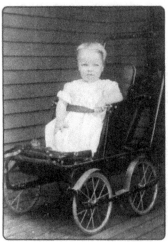

Frank Dillard (Dill) Payne, Jr.

S. B. (Bubba) Carter, left, and brother Van, 1928

William and Mae Templeman, 1926

Girtie Boyd Ranburger with sons, Dorris and Norris Hightower

Maxine Latham with Albert Greenfield's 1940 Chevrolet, 1944

Senior Class Officers, 1966, Todd Central: Bobby Gower, Don Wilkins, Laverne Gregory, Mary Sue DeLozier, Lynn Case

Road grading with a team of horses, 1940

From left: William, Carl, Orene, and Mae Templeman, 1930

Matthew Sherrod, Sr., and Bill McElvain, Guthrie, KY

Brothers James E., Jr., Samuel F., and Ewing E. Farmer with their 1935 Plymouth. June 1940

From left: Louise, Bob, Irene and Sarah Luttrull

Car belonging to Virgil Harrison, Nov. 6, 1950

Trenton street scene at the corner of Hwy. 104 and North Main Street. The old hotel, Trenton House, is in the background.

South Main street in Trenton, KY

Robert "Bob" Fortson, fireman with L&N Railroad Company, and others pose by train in Guthrie, Kentucky

Rainey Moore

Train leaving the Elkton Station with Olis Simpson Welborn and friends in 1916

Resting on the running board of a Model T truck, smoking their "stogies," circa 1920

Charles and Lelia Nabb and grandson Allen Poke standing by their 1932 Hupmobile dressed for the Sesquicentennial.

Virgil Petrie (on horse) and others working on Highway 181 in the 1920's

Bob Payne and sister, Sarah Payne Bouldin, 1950

Spurlin Cobb at home on a visit from the Navy in 1964 in his 1958 Chevy convertible.

Dunnie Fortson and Grace Wilson, made at the Fortson home on State St., Guthrie, KY

Romie Gant and daughter, Dorothy Jean, with their automobile, probably a 1925 Ford

Man on the left is Billy Ware

Kinney's Service Center, Elkton, KY, 1967. Billy Star Jones and Joe Lynn Altman (Randall Miller in background)

New to us: Mrs. Joe (Sue) Brown sits in their first car, a 1950 Studebaker, bought used from Mr. B. G. Harris, a prominent Sharon Grove citizen. Sharon Grove Feed Mill in the background. Note the telephone pole with the overhead lines

K 1 Late Model Stockcar, driver David Miller

1958 photo of Joe Brown and his 1957 Chevy two door - black and white with red interior (note the fender skirts)

Mr. Maynor Nabb at the back of their T-Model Ford in the 1920's

BUSINESSES

Francis Dorris by the Telephone Office in Sharon Grove, KY, 1936

J.W. Cook building in Guthrie, KY

Crossroads in Sharon Grove, KY, 1903

Norma Adams Meriwether and friends

Car on street in Sharon Grove, KY, 1936

Sharon Grove Feed Mill, built in early 1930's by the Charlie Moore Family as a flour mill, which made meal and Red Bird Flour. It was operated several years by different members of the family. Some lived in the side room. Others that have owned and operated it were Jesse Sanders, John Borders, B. G. Harris, Coleman Oglesby, Brent and Dalton Hinton, Buna Brown (Joe's dad), Jim Spencer along with Joe Brown, who have had a partnership in it since 1954. He and his wife, Sue, still own the building, although it is no longer in operation.

Wright's Store in Sharon Grove, KY, 1936

Wallace (Buzz) Bell, 1953, Bell Motor Company, Elkton, KY

Vina Heltsley Hightower in front of Riley Heltsley's Grocery in Clifty, 1952

Louise Gossett standing in show window of Hamilton's Drug Store, Guthrie, KY

Dr. J. C. Woodall in his office at Trenton, Kentucky

In Honor: Woodmen of the World, Lewisburg, KY, Lodge 574 held a flag presentation ceremony Sept. 11, 2002 at the Sharon Grove Volunteer Fire Department, presenting them with a flag and flagpole dedicated in memory of the many firefighters and others who lost their lives Sept. 11, 2001 at the World Trade Center/Pentagon disaster. Approximately 50 people attended, including state and county officials, W.O.W. members, firefighters and local citizens.

NUMBER PLEASE. Seated at the switchboard front: Fairleigh Woods, Alma Carter. Standing, from left: Lucy Lawson, Marcus Graves, Barbara Cole, and Mary Dickinson. The office went to dial and closed August 20, 1955 (date of picture)

Stagecoach Inn, 88 Graysville Road, Guthrie, Ky, home of Steve and Shelton Meriwether

Dr. and Mrs. George Brown in front of the Todd County Animal Clinic

Guthrie Hardware Store, 1947

Rust's Grocery, Penchem, KY, owned and operated by Roland and Martha Rust, from the late 1940s until the late 1960's.

Ladies' Writing Room at the Trenton, KY, Post Office

Downtown Guthrie depicts the grand opening of W. E. Rogers' grocery and hardware stores about 1912. The grocery store is on the right. The site of the stores was on the west side of Ewing Street, where the woodworking shop is currently housed. From the late 1930's until 1962, part of the building housed the Guthrie Post Office. W. E. Rogers was not only a businessman, he was also a political leader who did much for the city of Guthrie. He served as City Judge from 1904 to 1912, as State Representative in 1914, and as a State Senator in 1916. In 1933 he was again elected to the House of Representatives and served as Speaker in 1934 and 1935. He was instrumental in securing a water works for Guthrie and for persuading the state to pave the gravel road that is now route 364, connecting Guthrie to Highway 79.

Glascock's Grocery, from left: Bill Chesnut, R.O. Glascock

W. L. Kimbrough & Son Hardware Store window

Trenton Milling Company

Guthrie Garage service truck. Note the Lyric Theater in the background

Guthrie, KY, 1918

First Truck: Joe and Sue Brown by their 1953, 3/4 ton Chevy pickup truck that was used for hauling and delivering feed for the Sharon Grove Feed Mill. The mill owned and operated by the Brown's and her father, Jim Spencer. Neal Heltsley was a longtime employee.

Nellie Ruth Camp in front of Trenton Hardware

Left: Margie Escue, Ruth Boisseau and Tenie Borders at Sharon Grove telephone office, 1915

Addison Trucking Company, owned and operated by William Addison for 52 years. After retirement sold business to Jeff Lear. Right: Certificate of Achievement presented to Addison

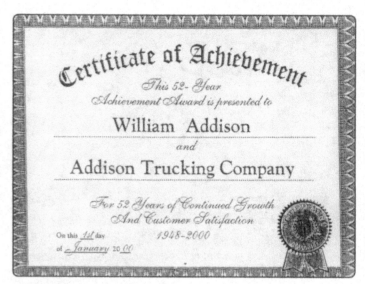

Eleanor Crossman posing on street in Guthrie, KY

Barbara Hurt standing in front of the Todd Theatre in Elkton, KY

Bill Longhurst standing in doorway of Longhurst General Store, est. 1937

Potato Chip bag from Allen's Specialty Company, Trenton, KY

Virgil Petrie Store, Clifty. In operation over 100 years; later used as the U. S. Post Office. Edna Petrie was the last to use this building in her role as Post Mistress.

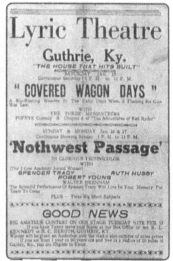

Theatre poster/Lyric Theatre, Guthrie, KY. (They misspelled words then, too.)

W. L. (Jack) Breakfield, 1945, owner of Grocery and Hardware Store for 55 years in Allensville, KY

Delivery trucks for Allen's Specialty Company.

Left: Tom Bellar, August 1967, Guthrie, KY

POSTCARDS

Elkton Fair Grounds, located behind Vanderbilt Training School, present location of Todd Middle School. Circa 1910

Post card advertising Harvest Moon Motel and Cafe, located 1/2 mile west on U. S. Hwy 80, Elkton. Has 11 fireproof stone units, modern in every way, air cooled. One stop service for gas and oil. Fine food in Cafe. Open from 5:00 A. M. to 11: 30 P. M. Owned and operated by Mr. and Mrs. E. Y. Hurt. Taxi cab operated by Felix J. Spottswood is parked in front

Postcard from Bank of Allensville, dated June 16, 1926, advising customer that $215.27 had been deposited to their account

Postcard advertising Covington Motel, circa 1950's. On U.S. Highway 41, Guthrie, KY, 28 modern units, tile baths, tub and showers, thermostatically controlled electric heat. Air conditioned and city water. Excellent restaurant across the street.

Postcard advertising the historic Stage Coach Inn, located at intersection of U. S. 41 & 79, Guthrie. Established in early 1800's. Visited by many notable persons including Jenny Lind, Andrew Jackson, Jesse James. Excellent meals, southern hospitality. Tuesday thru Saturday 11 A. M.-P. M., Sunday Noon - 9 P. M. Closed Monday. Authentic antiques. Owned and operated by Mr. and Mrs. Thad Northington

Postcard advertising The Coffee Cup Restaurant, circa 1950's. Intersection of U. S. 41 and 70, Tiny Town, KY (near Guthrie). Traditional Kentucky hospitality and southern cooking featured. Rib-eye steaks a specialty. Attractive gift items available in new additional dining room. Both service station and restaurant give the traveling public 24 hour service.

Bethel Baptist Church, Fairview, circa 1960's. The church stands where the original Davis home stood at the time of Jefferson Davis' birth in 1808.

Postcard advertising Tiny Town, KY, circa 1950's. One stop tourist accomadations, 24 hour service. Air-conditioned motel, super service station, air-conditioned restaurant.

Russellville Street looking east from the Elkton Public Square, circa 1910. On the left is the Jefferson Davis Hotel and on the right is C. E. Rogers Drug Store. The steeple of the Baptist Church can be seen in the background.

Southeast corner of Elkton Public Square, circa 1900. Businesses shown include C. E. Rogers Drug Store, C. M. Redford Grocery, John N. Williams Company, Boone & Williams Grocery. The second building after turning the corner was the location of Boone and Sons' Dry Goods.

Elkton Graded School, located on Washington Street, was built in 1888 and used as a school until 1925. This postcard picture, circa 1890's, was taken by J. B. Settle. The building was later used as a chicken hatchery and then an apartment building. As a result of a fire in 1987, the building was destroyed.

Mr. Joe Waller's Shop, Trenton

Right: Postcard advertising Covington's Tourist Court. 1/4 mile west of Guthrie, Kentucky, Route 41E. Modern steam heated cabins, private baths. 24-hr service.

Todd County Court House, circa 1960

Main Building of Vanderbilt Training School. Later became Elkton High School

Postcard of house in "Historic Old Graysville." Graysville is now known as Tiny Town.

Home of Robert A. Hardwick on Russellvile Street, Elkton, circa 1910. Current location of the Garden Shop of Haley Hardware. Mr. Hardwick worked many years for Boone and Sons' Dry Goods and was an active member of Petrie Memorial United Methodist Church.

The Elkton Christian Church, built 1912, is located on the corner of East Main and Perry Streets. The house to the right is the present home of Mr. and Mrs. Aubrey Campbell. The church parsonage was not built on the lot between the church and the Campbell house until 1947.

View of Todd County Court House from Hopkisnville Street, November 16, 1941.

Jefferson Davis Monument, circa 1950's

Entrance to Jefferson Davis Monument, circa 1960's

Bruce Boyd and Forest Hubbert

Trenton, KY, Post Office. From left: E. C. Stockwell, Postmaster, and his dog "Billie Gower," R.A. Williams, R.J. Chiles, L.J. Basford, Roy L. Basford, W. M. Hirshfeld, Asst. Postmaster

Gathering on Main Street, Trenton

Milliken Memorial Community House, circa 1950

Davis Restaurant located next to the Lyric Theater, Guthrie, KY

Left: Bethel Baptist Church, Fairview, KY. Jefferson Davis was born on this site June 3, 1808

SPECIAL STORIES

HARRY WEBSTER PETERS AND IVA GRACE SOLOMON PETERS

Peters' Administration, 1936-1940

Harry Webster Peters, the twenty-fifth Superintendent of Public Instruction of Kentucky, was born October 18, 1893, at Rushville, Roan County, West Virginia, the son of Lewis K. and Melissa Meadows Peters. At the age of nine, with his parents, he came to Marshall County, Kentucky, where he enjoyed fishing, swimming, shooting, and the freedom of the farm. He often refers to his boyhood experiences "down on the creek."

H.W. Peters

He received his early education at "Rush Creek School" in Roane County, West Virginia, which had been taught by his father, grandfather and others of his ancestry. After his parents moved to Kentucky he attended the schools of Marshall County - "Oak Hill" and others. He graduated from the Western Kentucky State Teachers College with a B. S. degree. At Western Kentucky State Teachers College, where he did supervisory work for the College, Mr. Peters became an ardent admirer of his personal friend, Henry Hardin Cherry, who was President of that institution from its beginning until his death in 1937. The advice, friendship and inspiration that President Cherry gave Harry Peters undoubtedly greatly influenced his future.

On December 24, 1921, Mr. Peters was married to Iva Grace Solomon of Calvert City, Kentucky. Before her marriage, Mrs. Peters was an excellent teacher, and had rendered valuable assistance to Mr. Peters in his school work. They have three children, Lewis Lee, Mary Jane, and William Webster.

One of the outstanding characteristics of Mr. Peters is his business-like management of both his personal and public affairs. No only he, but each member of his family, "budgets," and lives accordingly. By his management of the finances of Marshall and Christian County school systems, he captured the attention and respect of educa-

tional leaders. It was this ability which made leaders predict early in his career that he would rise to the Superintendency of Public Instruction in Kentucky. He further attracted attention as superintendent of county schools when he became one of the first in his section to see and want the advantages of consolidation and larger school units for the people he served so capably. His work in his county sparked in him a desire for school consolidation throughout Kentucky.

Mr. Peters is a member of the Methodist Church, the Masonic faternity, and the Kiwanis Club (Hopkinsville and Frankfort).

Iva Grace Solomon Peters, daughter of Leander Solomon and Delcona Foust, natives of Marshall County. Educated in Benton High School and Western Teachers College. She has been an active member of the Methodist Church for fifty-five years, and taught

Iva Grace Solomon Peters

three rural schools before her marriage to Harry Webster Peters, son of Lewis Karnes Peters and Melissa Jane Meadows, natives of Roane County, West Virginia. Mrs. Peters is the mother of Lewis Lee, William Webster, and Mary Jane Peters (Mrs. Clifton Durrett Camp), all of whom are college trained. The grandmother of Lewis Christian, Melissa Jane, William Gunnar and Elizabeth Jane Peters, Daniel Durrett, Thomas Clifton, Pamela Jane and Emily Ann Camp. She and her husband have always been interested in public education and he is a

former Superintendent of Public Instruction of Kentucky. Mrs. Peters has always participated in community affairs for public welfare she has a unique understanding of problems facing the average citizen concerning home, church, and community and has served as chairman of committees and president of many community organizations. She served ten years (1954 to 1964) as State of Kentucky for the American Mothers Committee, Inc., and was a National Vice-Chairman of the Young Mothers Council Service of the American Mothers Committee. She was appointed National Organizer for Kentucky by the Federated Grandmother Clubs of America. Mrs. Peters was awarded a citation for her pioneering efforts in developing the young Mothers Council Service in her state, and for the book *Mothers of Kentucky,* a brief history of the American Mothers Committee in the Blue Grass State. Her hometown honored her in 1965 by proclaiming an "Iva Peters Day" in Trenton. She was nominated by the members of the Grandmother Club of Trenton No. 397. Her advice to young mothers is to begin the job of training their children early in life and according to her the mission of the mothers of today is "to make the whole world homelike".

Guthrie Elementary School's second grade took their annual historical tour of Todd County on May 17, 1988 . They visited the Robert Penn Warren birthplace and Stage Coach Inn, had story time during the visit to the library in the historical Todd County Courthouse, and then ate lunch at the Jefferson Davis State Park.

Ad appearing in the monthly publication, Soothsayer, by the students of the Elkton Public High School, 1920

GENIE CORNS HAS SPECIAL REASON TO APPRECIATE INDEPENDENCE DAY

Genie Corns was born and lived in Germany during the time of Hitler's rule. She was five years old when war came to her town and her family and took the father away to serve in Hitler's army. Her father was a photographer and movie producer by trade. Her mother was a nurse and Genie was the youngest of four children. She remembers running and hiding when the air raid warning came, and they came frequently. She remembers not having enough food, neighbors losing adult family members as well as children. When the war was over and her father returned and life returned to some form of normalcy, all was not as well as it appeared. Genie was malnourished and sent to a health camp, where she didn't speak a word for the six weeks that she was there.

After the war attitudes changed, all except for Genie's daddy and he just didn't like that GI that kept coming to their house, obviously smitten with his daughter, and so Genie and James dated for over eighteen months, married when she was 22 and left Germany a year later, when Corn's duty was discharged. They found the house of their dreams in Guthrie.

"You just have to put some things behind you and go on. Life goes on and so must you. She became an American citizen in May of 1968.

As the Fourth of July came and went, she remembers the past, enjoys the present, and looks forward to the future. She wishes that all Americans better understood and appreciated the freedom that abounds in this great country.

PETER T. WRIGHT
NOVEMBER 18, 1946 - MAY 8, 2000

Accomplished photographer, Peter Wright, returned to this area, where he had spent several years during his childhood, to be near his father, Buck Wright, of Trenton. During the late 1970s and through the 1980s Wright was an award winning photo-journalist for *The Associated Press*; he brought an impressive portfolio when he joined the staff of *The Kentucky New Era*, in Hopkinsville, Kentucky, in December 1995, as chief photographer. Wright shared a log home on the banks of the West Fork of the Red River in Trenton, with his companion and friend Linda Jolly. He continued capturing images on film that often could take your breath away, and did some of his best photographic work during his years at the new Era.

In Peter's own words, "On a beautiful fall day many years ago, my grandfather took me fishing on a creek on his farm.

As he cast his line into the water, I would wander around the bank picking up stones and skip them across the top of the water,

Two horses kick up some dust in a dry pond bed on the farm of David A. Grace, near Gracey, Kentucky, Aug. 25, 1999

making all the noise a youngster could make, not aware of how this would scare the fish away from his line.

My grandfather never got upset with me, even when I would wade into the water to collect leaves that would flow down the stream and cascade over the rocks. When we were ready to head back to the house, he picked up one of them from the stack I had gathered and carried it home and placed it into a book.

After he passed away, I was going through some old books that had been boxed up and came across the one with the leaf and it brought back a flood of memories of that day I spent with him.

By placing it in that book, my grandfather had captured a moment in time that will stay with me as long as I live.

Photography is the same thing as placing a leaf into a book - it is a moment frozen in time. Every time you snap the shutter on a camera, you have captured a moment in history. It might be a photo of your kids playing with a new puppy or just that new car in the driveway.

I have been told how much people like my photos and I have also been called a low-down dirty jerk for some of the photos I have taken over the years. It would be great if I could just take photos of kids playing, but with my job also comes the fact that I have to take photos that show the harsh reality of life. It's not a part of my work that I enjoy but it is my job to capture that moment in time by the click of a shutter." From *The Kentucky New Era*.

Two Mennonite children use tree branches to help volunteer firemen beat down a fire in a newly harvested cornfield south of Fairview on Sept. 30, 1997. The fire, which started while workers were applying fertilizer to the field, burned about 50 acres of corn stubble. (One photo of this fire was nominated for a Pulitzer Prize.)

Peter Wright with Paula Cobb behind him. "Who would have known he would photograph Presidents?"

Charles (Chess) McCartney, referred to as the "Goat Man," was an eccentric wanderer who traveled through this area every spring from his home in Georgia on his way to visit relatives in Iowa. It is believed that his pilgrimages through here started in the late 1930's; he was coming annually through here, with his entourage of wagon-pulling goats, in the 1940's and early into the 1950's. He almost always walked instead of riding on his goat wagon during his cross country treks, and he drew a lot of attention from the natives while resting here. (The old goat wagon is now in a museum in Florida.) Taken from The Kentucky New Era

Kent Greenfield, Guthrie, Kentucky, most successful rooky pitcher of 1925. Pitched for the New York Giants during the 1925 season. Photo from the Todd County Standard, *1976*

THREE SMITH DAUGHTERS

William Dabney and Mary Elizabeth Tandy came to Todd County from Louisa County, Virginia, in 1837 with Dabney Smith, William's father. They settled about three miles south of Trenton on a farm that they named Breezewood. They had eight children, three of whom were daughters.

Life was hard enough for them, but the year of 1878-1879 proved to be very tragic. All three daughters died during childbirth.

The middle daughter was Mary Beauford. She was married to Charles G. Massie of Christian County. She died during the birth of her son, Hugh, in November 1878. Hugh was raised by his grandmother Massie.

The second death came just four months later in February of 1879. Irene Helon married William Randle Jr. She had a daughter named Irene Beauford on February 28, 1879. Irene Helon died of blood loss. The baby, Irene Beauford, was raised by William Dabney and Elizabeth Smith at Breezewood. She grew up and married Lucien Camp. They had two children, Elisabeth and Lucien. Elisabeth, better know as Libba Russell, lived in Elkton, Kentucky. Lucien married, but neither he nor Elisabeth had any

children.

The last duaghter was Eliza Ashton who was always called Ashton. She married George T. Cross in 1878 in a double wedding with her sister, Irene Helon. The wedding took place in the family home, Breezewood. In 1879, mother, Eliza Ashton

and daughter both died during chilbirth. The baby daughter is buried with her mother in the Smith plot on the farm.

All three Smith daughters are buried in the family cemetery. Breezewood is presently home to the seventh generation of Smiths.

Picture of home on page 83.

Smith daughters - all three daughters died in childbirth

AUNT LUCY

*Although this picture is not in color, the original had been tinted. You might think the entire picture would be tinted with color but only Aunt Lucy's dress. Aunt Lucy was my aunt by marriage to my Father's brother, Paul Chastain. She had beautiful red hair, and always tried to wear colors that were becoming to a red head. I was looking through her pictures one day, when she came to this picture. "My, my, I must make a note on this picture," which she did. On the back of the picture is written: Daddy & me, Made in 1924. I never had a **pink** dress. L.F.C.*

Blue and Grey Camp operated by the WPA Recreation Division for under-priviledged children (Housing for workers, 1940)

Courthouse repaired by WPA, Feb 25,-May 17, 1937

First person buried in the Gant cemetery, Zachariah "Zack" Gant. Born in 1774.

Grave marker at Gants Cemetery for Fannie Shelton and Thomas Jefferson Dorris

MARY LIZZIE OF TRENTON

One particular telephone in Trenton, Kentucky, is constantly ringing. The caller invariably needs assistance in some way. Whether it be a sick relative, an elderly shut-in or just simply a mother with children who need a baby sitter, they have called the right person. The person? Mary Lizzie, of course. To every citizen in the small town of Trenton, Mary Lizzie Trice is a 52 year old wonder worker.

Mary Lizzie Trice was born in Trenton and has lived there all her life. She has made an impression on her own town so lasting that the city fathers bestowed a plaque in pure appreciation upon her a short time ago. The plaque refers to the many kind and generous deeds of Mary Lizzie.

Except for this small item of special recognition, Mary Lizzie has only the smiles and thanks of her many friends and neighbors as recognition for her endless energy. But to Mary Lizzie this is more than enough. In fact, she does not ask for special treatment, she just likes to help other people.

Helping other people has become a lifelong career for this big hearted lady. Since helping her older sister care for their younger brothers and sisters after their mother died, Mary Lizzie knew what she wanted to do. Her dream was to care for children whenever she could. Mary Lizzie liked to watch them grow. Her dreams have come true as she has helped raise almost every child in Trenton for thirty years. Even now, mothers know that Mary Trice is more than willing to babysit for them if she hasn't already committed herself. Not only does she love children but she also goes out of her way to help the sick and elderly of her home town.

Many people have great plans to love and help their neighbors but few ever practice their principles with such a fervor as Mary Lizzie Trice.

Ads appearing in the monthly publication, Soothsayer, by the students of the Elkton Public High School, 1920

Old newspaper column - "Flapper Fanny Says:"

Todd County Hatchery postcard ad in 1936

Cooling off - Matt Krupp (from left), Parker Cole, Kyle Penick and Conrad Reding jump off bluffs while swimming in the Little West Fork of the Red River Wednesday near the Todd-Christian County line. New Era/Peter Wright.

DOROTHY DIX

If I could give one piece of advice more earnest than any other to the young man about to be married, it would be this: Keep your wife busy. See to it that she has plenty of real, honest-to-goodness, worthwhile work to do, and put some heart interest in her work by paying for it with both money and appreciation

Dorothy Dix - introduction to a column that she wrote for newspapers.

PARKER D. BELL DIES AT 69

Services for Parker D. Bell, 69, Trenton, were held at 3:30 p.m. Thursday, April 8 at Maddux Funeral Home in Pembroke with the Revs. Wayne Lyle and John R. Christian officiating. Burial was in Edgewood Cemetery, Trenton.

Mr. Bell died at 1 p.m. Tuesday, April 6, 1976 at Jennie Stuart Hospital after a long illness.

A native of Wayne County, he was born may 16, 19096, the son of Henry Clay and Nannie Cooper Bell. He was a retired rural mail carrier at Trenton and a member of the Christian Church.

Survivors include his widow, Mrs. Belle Maynard Bell; one son, Henry M. Bell, Baton Rouge, La.; four sisters, Mrs. Raas Vaughn,

Mayfield, Mrs. Asher L. Young, Nashville, Tenn., and Mrs. Joe Orr and Mrs. Lon Slaughter, both of Bowling Green; and three grandsons.

One brother preceded him in death.

Mr. Bell began his career as a mail carrier in 1939, using a one horse buggy on his rounds. In 1943 he purchased an A-Model from the Norfleet Brothers in Trenton. On June 30, 1973, 34 years from the day he started carrying the mail, he retired. The following poem was written about him by Nancy Glascock Sneed, a longtime neighbor.

Pap

He was an honest man. You never had to guess where you stood on anything with him.

He was a truthful man. But his truth was softened by a touch of humor.

He was a man with a talent for making others see the funny side of life and themselves.

He was Trenton's own Will Rogers. And loved to spin a yarn or hear one equally well.

He was a man who loved nature. And was contented and at peace when out in the woods listening to the hounds run.

He was a lover of people. Thank you God for the opportunity we all had to love…and be loved by him.

(Newspaper article, April 8, 1976)

Down Memory Lane - Claymour School, 1914. Front row: unidentified, Alfred Hurt, Coleman Shemwell, Mable Kennedy, Aubrey Wright, Flora Boley, Mendrel Mallory, Elvia Morris, John Wright, unidentified, Merrill Heltsley, Ailene Nealy, Raymond Compton; second row: Lillian Morris, Owen Hurt, Felix Hightower, Eva Mallory, Cecil Borders, Thelma Gorrell, Claud Hightower, Nannie Marshall, unidentified, Hazel Stratton, Sidney Gorrell, Ara Lee Heltsley, Clarence Heltsley, Velma Robey, Kelly Hurt, Clara Duncan; third row: Roy Heltsley, Mary Knight, Walton Boley, Eupha Lee Shemwell, unidentified, Tina Boley, Ernest McBride, Carrie Wolfe, Key Hurt, Erna Robey, Bernis Wright, Perley Hurt, Guy Crowder, Hazel Duncan, Yergens Hurt, Odie Hightower; fourth row: Ellis Boley, Ray Hurt, Maurice Heltsley, Iola Wright, Edgar Hurt, Pauline Wright, Robert Compton, Willie Marshall, Arthur Jones, Miss Madie Bell (teacher), Annie Boley, Herbert Robey, Lou Heltsley, Ernest Gorrell, Marie Wright, Herbert Compton, Charlie Wolfe.

IN LOVING MEMORY OF
LUCY FORTSON CHASTAIN
"AUNT LUCY"
1911-2003

Aunt Lucy was our aunt and a friend to many others. Her main interests were her church, children, and cards.

She began her teaching career in July 1934 at the Hadensville School until 1936, a school in Mississippi (1936-1939), Allensville School (1939-1940), Elkton School (1940-1944 and 1949-1956), Trenton School (1948) and Guthrie School (1956-1972), retiring after 35 and one-half years of teaching experience.

She became our aunt by marriage to Paul Chastain. Aunt Lucy and Uncle Paul had one son, Mike Chastain, who was born April 12, 1945. Aunt Lucy took a four year break when Mike was born.

Aunt Lucy was a creative thinker. She always strived to make school an interesting and exciting place for children. Buying land as an investment for the future was a passion of hers. She was an excellent business woman with an enthusiasm for travel. She made many trips abroad and shared her knowledge in her classroom. She had her Masters Degree in Education, but then so did her mother, Nannie Fortson.

Pride in her immediate family as well as all children, regardless of their age, made her life complete. Reading to children was her delight. Any child that ever heard her read *Brer Rabbit* will never forget that voice. Her enthusiasm for young educators and administrators was evident by her steady encouragement, because she had been there and experienced most situations of daily school life.

Aunt Lucy shared her reading skill as a volunteer at South Todd and played Bridge with her buddies until she moved to Hearthstone, Elkton, Kentucky.

Most of the children that had Aunt Lucy as a teacher realized she had an indisputable love and interest in their well-being. She is genuinely missed, but she "poked many holes in the darkenss" for students in her care.

Sincerely,
Lelia Chastain Cole (niece)
Smith Chastain (nephew)
June Overton Hyndman (friend)

In Loving Memory

Glover Williams
1927-2003

People will recall Glover Williams as a determined, caring, supportive man of vision.

He would quietly help anyone and anything that was good. People always laughed when they saw Glover's constant companion, Peppy, a 6 pound Shih Tzu, standing beside his 6-foot-4 frame. He was so kind and sweet to her. It sums it up. He was compassionate about many things - big and small.

Williams, a 1945 Trenton High School graduate, was an aerographer's mate in the U.S. Navy aboard the *USS Fargo*. He was also the former production manager at *The Leaf-Chronicle*, Clarksville, Tennessee, retiring after 42 years with the company.

In his civic life, Glover had been all things to Trenton, his home town. He was a former mayor pro-tem, city councilman, fire chief, police chief and volunteer fireman. He had a love for Trenton and its people.

In December 2003 he was honored by the city of Trenton and the Kentucky General Assembly for his more than 50 years of community service.

A Kentucky Colonel and a Kentucky Admiral, Williams was a 32nd degree Mason and 50 year member of Bethel Lodge No. 204 F&AM in Trenton, having served as secretary. He was past president and a 50-year member of the Shrine's Rizpah Temple in Madisonville, KY. He was a member of Royal Order of Jesters, Pennyrile Court No. 171.

Glover is remembered fondly by wife Betty, three children, and five grandchildren.

The Williams Family

TRIBUTE TO DADDY

Wilbur Clark Cole
Trenton, Kentucky
1910-1962

Wilbur purchased Thompson-McChesney Hardware Store in July, 1944, after moving to Trenton from Bowling Green, Kentucky, Warren County. He boarded for several months with Guy and Lucy Lawson until he purchased the J.S. Dickinson home at 364 South Main Street.

In September, 1944, Wilbur moved his family. His wife, Gladys, sons, Hollis, Sheridan, and Barry came to their new home. In July, 1947, an addition of a twelve year old girl, niece of Gladys, Lorraine Gilliam, came to be a part of their family. Lorraine's father had passed away, and her mother was terminally ill. With all boys, Lorraine was a joyful addition to the family, a sister they would never have. Because in 1952 there was an addition of yet another baby boy, Terry Michael. *According to Sheridan, they were too old to have a baby. Terry had grandchild status and was spoiled rotten!*

Wilbur moved the Thompson-McChesney Hardware Store to a larger location for a few years and then built his own Trenton Hardware-Massy Ferguson Dealership building. He remained there until his health failed and sold the business to Ben Taylor and sons from Hopkinsville, KY.

Wilbur served on the Todd County School Board when they purchased the land to build Todd Central High School. He was a trustee of the Trenton Methodist Church during the construction of the current building after the rock church burned.

Although Daddy died at 51 years of age, (we thought he was old), he accomplished many things that he desired. He had a family and business in a small community that he loved. He enjoyed contributing to the community by volunteer service, and set an example that we have grown to respect and admire. We have missed him for many years, but when thoughts of him return, we smile.

Sheridan Lee Cole
Terry Michael Cole

B.R. (BILLY) KNUCKLES
1946-1995

B.R. (Billy) Knuckles, founder of B.R. Knuckles Insurance Agency in Elkton, Kentucky, was born in Muhlenberg County on July 25, 1946, the son of Audie E. and Sue Whitaker Knuckles. He lived in Logan County where he grew up with three brothers, Bobby, Wayne and Jerry. He attended school at Gordonsville, then graduated from Olmstead High School in 1964.

He and his wife, the former Barbara Burchett, also of Logan County, moved to Todd County in 1967 after the birth of their first child, Kenneth. The move was facilitated by Billy's job as an insurance salesman with Life and Casualty Insurance Company. In 1969 their second son, Johnny, was born. The family bought a home in the Daysville Community in 1973, where they still lived at the time of Billy's death on August 10, 1995.

In 1975, Billy opened B.R. Knuckles Insurance Agency at its initial location on North Main Street. Since 1983 to the present time, the location is at 55 Public Square in the historic building once occupied by the 1888 Bank of Elkton and previously owned by Mr. George Street Boone.

The insurance agency continues to be a successful business in the community, with both Barbara and Johnny involved as agents and managers. In addition to the insurance business, Billy also had worked for the U.S. Postal Service as a rural letter carrier in Todd County for several years. He was an active member of Elkton Baptist Church, an officer of the Optimist Club, and served on the Selective Service Board.

While in the insurance industry, he received several awards for his achievements. He enjoyed his work with and for the people in Todd County. Both of his sons and their families still reside in the county.

WEATHERS DRUGS

PROUD TO SERVE
TODD COUNTY SINCE 1875
(270)265-2155

EVELYN BOONE

THANK YOU
FOR ALL YOUR HARD WORK FOR TODD COUNTY!

A TRIBUTE TO DEAR HEARTS AND GENTLE PEOPLE
CHARLES AND ISABELLE ADAMS GLASCOCK

*"I love those dear hearts and gentle people
Who live in my home town
Because those dear hearts and gentle people
Will never, ever let you down."*

So go the words to an old song that occasionally runs through our minds. That song had to have been written about Trenton, Kentucky, because the people in that song are people like our parents, Charles and Isabelle Glascock and the friends and neighbors we remember from childhood.

Our parents are two life-long residents of Trenton, Kentucky, who happen to be man and wife. Charles Glascock was born in town on January 17, 1918, while our mother, Isabelle Adams was born June 21, 1919, out in the country just a few miles from Trenton.

Both were educated in Trenton and were high school sweethearts.

Charles and Isabelle married on March 3, 1940, set up housekeeping and proceeded to raise two daughters on Main Street in Trenton. Charles was in the grocery business with his father and brother; a business from which he retired in 1982.

Isabelle worked at various jobs for a few years before she found her niche in Trenton's Post Office.

Both have been active, supporting members of the community, involved in everything from church work and bridge clubs to selling raffle tickets and working the door at the Halloween Carnival to Charles' several terms as Fire Chief of Trenton's volunteer fire department.

Neither have ever considered living anywhere else, because there simply was no place better to live!

We are products of the Trenton Community and of Charles and Isabelle Glascock. In our opinion, no better childhoods could have existed!

May this page be a tribute to small town living, Trenton style, and to Charles and Isabelle Glascock, who continue to love their neighbors and Trenton, Kentucky.

*Proudly and lovingly submitted by
Nancy Glascock Sneed
Tracy Glascock Holman*

JAMES H. ANDERSON

In the spring of 1940, a young Trenton boy boarded a bus bound for a very uncertain future. He could not fathom the significance of the events that would unfold before him.

We are proud of our father, Jim Anderson, for many things, but especially for his exemplary war career. He joined the Army at the age of twenty, and his unit, the 7th Infantry of the Third Army, was constantly engaged with the German Army. He moved from French Morocco and Tunisia to the invasion of North Africa. From there, they went to Sicily and Southern Italy. He survived the brutal and horrible battle of Anzio. They then moved to French Riviera and the Rhine Campaigns. Next came the German Campaign, the dash into Salzburg, Austria, and the capture of Berchtesgaden, Germany.

The Third Army inflicted more casualties on the German Army than any other unit. They also had the most decorations and the most Medal of Honor winners. Sergeant Anderson was engaged in seven major campaigns and made five beach landings in the European Theatre. It was quite an adventure for a country boy. It changed him in many ways. He often said that the war made him appreciate the importance of kindness. Among other honors, he was awarded the Bronze Star with V for valor, Combat Infantry Badge, two Purple Hearts and the French Croix de Guerre.

He is remembered for his kindness, his integrity, his love for the people of Trenton, and his love for his grandchildren.

Written in his honor by his children, Dick Anderson and Judy Anderson Donnelly

NED ARMISTEAD GLOVER
1932-2000

Study the lives of people you admire. See what made them tick - what their priorities were - what they cared about.

Ned Glover was born May 29, 1932, grew into an adult, and died on the land he loved and fought to preserve for generations of Glovers to come.

Who you are is about where you've come from and where you are going. Ned came from a family that loved education, land preservation, and family. He knew where he was going - right where he had always been, on the family farm off Cemetery Road in Trenton, Kentucky, on the banks of West Fork Creek. He remained in close contact with his brother, Robert, and two sisters, Pat and Linda.

Ned married Harriet Day Williams and fathered two sons, Robert and Ned Armistead, (Bubba).

Tobacco farming was a passion as well as Vanderbilt basketball. Being a Vandy fan in Kentucky wasn't easy.

His closeness to the earth probably strengthened his relationship with God. He was a life-long member of Mt. Zion Baptist Church where he was a deacon and song leader most of his adult life.

His friendly personality encouraged nicknames for family members and close friends. He remained true to the habits and traditions of his ancestors - *Loving, Laughing, and Singing.*

He will forever be missed by those that loved, laughed, and sang with him. Ned followed his heart as well as his head - *made a living, but more importantly made a life.*

Affectionately,
David and Patti Glover
Bubba and Jackie Glover

MARY KATHERINE SCOTT
"MAMMAM"
1924 - 1999

Love is patient, love is kind.
It does not envy, it does not boast, it is not proud.
It is not rude, it is not self seeking
It is not easily angered; it keeps no record of wrongs.
Love does not delight in evil but rejoices with the truth.
It always protects, always trusts,
Always perseveres.

1 Corinthians 13:4-7

Mary Katherine was our mother, grandmother, friend, and teacher. She blessed all of us with love, commitment, loyalty, and strength. She is sadly missed by her three "little girls," her grandchildren and their families - but our sweet memories of her will live forever.

MATT AND GRACE SHERROD

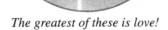

The greatest of these is love!

In memory and appreciation of Matt and Grace Sherrod by Paul Whitaker.

RICHARD TARLETON AVERITT, 1910 - 1999
OZELLA BLANCHE AVERITT, 1911 - 1997

GRANDPARENTS, PARENTS, TEACHERS, MENTORS, CARETAKERS, GODLY EXAMPLES...AND SO MUCH MORE!

Blanche and Tarleton Averitt married in 1934 in Stewart County, Tennessee. They moved to Trenton, Kentucky, in 1943 with their two daughters, Tommie and Sarah. The marriages of Tommie and Sarah produced six grandchildren and fourteen great-grandchildren.

Our mother and grandmother was a beautiful Godly woman that blessed us with her grace and style. She worked without ceasing or complaining in every area of her life. She was seldom idle. When picturing her in our minds, she was always working or reading her Bible or listening to Billy Graham on TV or the radio. She was always involved in the Trenton Baptist Church and set a pattern for us. As a homemaker, she was the best...from making biscuits or coconut cake to giving the perfect bridal shower. She was a true Southern Belle. We are all better people for having had her in our lives.

Our father and grandfather was the most influential person in our lives. He was the Monarch of the family. Without a doubt he was the wisest man we ever knew. He was bold when we needed discipline, security when we were afraid, funny when we needed a lift, knowledgeable when we needed advice, and a solid rock for our family. He gave to us an inheritance of character far above what we ever realized we had absorbed from him. We never knew him to be stingy with time or money when it came to his children or grandchildren. He was ALWAYS there when we needed him and is sorely missed. He taught us the Word of God by living it and serving the Trenton Baptist Church as an active deacon until retirement.

In loving tribute by daughters and granddaughters.

BRO. JOHN

John 3:16 is one of the favorite verses of a man who has dedicated his life in service to his community, church, and God. John Richard Christian, Bro. John as he is know to most, was born on Feb. 17, 1922 the son of Charlie and Lena Christian. As a young boy he attended the Methodist church with his mother. At the age of nine, he began attending the Baptist church with his father. Miss Mary Edloe Mimms, his Sunday School teacher, served cookies at the end of each class. Chocolate chip cookies were the first step in his becoming a Baptist minister.

Bro. John was educated in Trenton and graduated from Trenton High School in 1940, one of nine seniors. He went on to Austin Peay, received his Divinity Degree from Southern Theological Seminary, and a Master's Degree from Peabody. He was ordained a minister at Trenton Baptist Church on Aug. 2, 1942. His first pastorates were in Lafayette and Sinking Fork (1942-1947). Others included Oak Grove near Springfield (1947-63), First Baptist in Goodlettsville (1963-71), and the Second Church in Hopkinsville (1971-87). In 1987, he retired and moved back to his family farm in Trenton. His retirement was short, however, since he served as interim paston at Sinking Fork for the next 13 years. After sixty-one years in the ministry, he is now in his second retirement, but still serves as a supply pastor when needed.

Bro. John is often sought for advice because of his good decision making ability. Soon after becoming a minister he began dating a Pembroke girl named Kathleen Johnson. After they dated for a while, he developed a fancy for motorcycles. He decided to get one and take his best girl for a ride. Mrs. Johnson wasn't too happy about the idea and told him he had to choose between her daughter and the motorcycle. He chose the girl. That was without a doubt one of the best decisions he ever made. He and Kathleen were married on May 29, 1948. They are now happily enjoying their 55th year of marriage. One of the unique characteristics of Bro. John is his ability to witch water. Known as a dowser or "water witch," he takes two short, limber peach tree branches and crosses them at their ends. As he walks along, the branches will bend to the ground where there is water. He has never accepted a penny for his services. His reward has been the enjoyment he has gotten from helping others and the many friends he has made while "witching" a well.

Through the years, Bro. John has been a source of encouragement, inspiration, compassion, and counsel to many. He has a gifted voice that is pleasing to the ear and comforting to the soul. He has the ability of not only knowing what to say, but exactly how to say it. A talk with Bro. John is an uplifting and strengthening experience. He is a masterful story teller and loves to relate events that are mostly funny and always interesting. There is usually a message to be found somewhere in the story. Although he has received many honors and awards, he serves with great humility never seeking, wanting, or expecting any personal recognition. Many times he has been called on to conduct a funeral service for someone he has never met. He has made personal sacrifices to go at a moment's notice to comfort someone in time of need. While he performs his duties with humility and reverence, he loves a funny joke and is always looking for an opportunity to tease and enjoy a good laugh.

Bro. John's life reminds one of a story about another minister who served his entire life dedicated to helping others. He gave tirelessly and faithfully getting little appreciation for his efforts. On his retirement, he boarded a train and began the journey to his home town. As the train pulled in the station, there was a crowd of people, a marching band, and a podium with banners and welcome signs. The minister was overjoyed at the homecoming. When the train stopped, a well known politician stepped to the podium as the crowd cheered and the band played. Disappointed, the minister bowed his head realizing the celebration was not for him. Then he heard a voice saying, do not be discouraged. This trip was but a short journey in life and this stop but a pause in your service. After all, you are not all the way home yet. So it is in the life of Bro. John. One day his task on earth will be complete and his journey through this life will end. Those of us left here will be saddened with heavy hearts, but there will be joy and celebration in heaven. On that day, eyes will lift to the sky, ears will attune to heaven and in the distance a celestial orchestra will play, a choir of angels will sing, and the voices of those who have gone before will sound. Above all, a voice will be heard throughout heaven saying, Well done thou good and faithful servant. Welcome home, Bro. John.

On a personal note, I would like to add that Bro. John has touched and blessed my life many times and in many ways. He is a source of strength and guidance to my family. After all, he is part of my family. I am proud and yet at the same time humble to call him Uncle John.

Respectfully submitted with affection and admiration,
Mary Lee Dickinson McCuiston
November 2003

INDEX

GARDNERS
59
GARTH
76, 85, 94
GIBBS
57
GIFFORD
79
GILL
40, 92
GILLIAM
7, 32, 35, 40, 78, 119
GILLIS
84
GILLUM
43
GILMORE
33
GLASCOCK
5, 6, 33, 37, 39, 61, 63, 70, 74, 87, 103, 116, 123, 132
GLENN
15, 22, 23, 60, 81

GLOVER
23, 40, 46, 49, 59, 61, 65, 76, 77, 78, 92, 125
GOODING
94
GORRELL
16, 50, 60, 116
GOSSETT
56, 58, 101
GOWER
69, 88, 96
GRACE
111
GRAHAM
21, 31
GRAVES
36, 60, 101
GRAY
42, 43, 57, 69
GREEN
65, 78, 81, 133

GREENFIELD
5, 10, 11, 13, 17, 19, 25, 37, 69, 79, 96, 112
GREER
32
GREGORY
74, 96
GROVES
14, 93
GUINN
58, 69
GULAGER
56

H

HADDEN
9, 17, 29, 32, 40, 60
HAITHCOCK
41
HALEY
20, 42, 46, 65, 83, 136
HALL
16, 26, 29, 40, 43, 61

HAMBY
30
HAMLET
42, 72
HAMN
40
HAMPTON
69, 74, 76, 92
HANN
79
HARDWICK
107
HARPER
92
HARRELL
44
HARRIS
25, 40, 53, 87, 99, 100
HARRISON
8, 16, 19, 20, 22, 26, 28, 29, 38, 42, 84, 97
HATCHER
70, 74
HAUN
66
HEFLIN
31
HELTSLEY
16, 18, 19, 60, 87, 101, 103, 116
HENDERSON
39, 57, 92
HENSHAW
92
HIGGINS
39, 56, 75, 77
HIGHTOWER
4, 11, 53, 74, 78, 96, 101, 116
HILL
36, 64
HINES
3, 69
HINTON
100
HIRSHFELD
82, 108
HITLER
110
HOGAN
20, 23, 28, 64, 80, 84

Trenton High School Basketball Team, 1934-35. First row from left: Ward Mason, Herbert Adams, Graham Sweeney, Elliott Watts, Guy Nabb, Will Waller. Second row from left: Harold Hutcherson, Durward Anderson, Robert Hutcherson, Charles Glascock. Third row from left: Coach, James Henry Jones, Harry Williams, Murrey Moore, Bob Lawson

Cheerleaders-Bottom from left: Tina Patterson, Dora Nelson, Georgie Sumpter. Middle: Yvonne Green, Lisa Sadler. Top: Lisa Lewis

MARSHALL
116
MARTIN
9, 17, 29, 32, 56, 58, 69, 93
MASON
9, 132
MASSIE
112
MATHER
39
MAYER
12
MAYNARD
28, 57, 61, 70, 77, 85
MCAFEE
29, 32
MCALLEN
61
MCBRIDE
60, 116
MCCARTHY
76
MCCARTNEY
112
MCCHESNEY
119
MCCLANAHAN
36
MCCLENDON
47, 78
MCCLURE
79
MCCRERY
40
MCCROW
79
MCCUISTON
81, 129
MCDOUGAL
64
MCDOUGLE
88
MCELVAIN
97
MCELWAIN
12, 40, 63, 70
MCGHEE
29
MCINTOSH
5, 17, 40

MCKEEHAN
4
MCKINNEY
32
MCMURRAY
79
MCMURREY
46
MCMURRY
76, 79
MEADOWS
109
MENEES
73
MERIWETHER
45, 77, 83, 96, 100, 101
MILLEN
84
MILLER
4, 6, 16, 21, 22, 24, 25, 32, 36, 43, 48, 84, 91, 92, 99
MIMMS
70, 83, 129
MITCHELL
12, 24
MOBLEY
42
MONROE
64
MOODY
69, 76
MOORE
15, 16, 69, 71, 86, 98, 100, 132
MORGAN
60, 69, 76
MORHEAD
53
MORRIS
116
MOSELEY
24
MOSS
50
MOULTON
79
MUDGE
57
MULLINS
77

MUNGER
53
MURPHY
70, 74
MURREY
40, 78
MURRY
69

N

NABB
45, 61, 70, 74, 98, 99, 132
NAIVE
32
NEALY
116
NELSON
69, 76, 133
NEWCOMB
65, 78
NEWTON
69
NIXON
11, 37
NOBLE
40
NOEL
64
NORFLEET
116
NORTHERN
85, 89
NORTHING
74
NORTHINGTON
11, 13, 70, 76, 105

O

OFFUTT
29
OGLESBY
100
O'HARA
76
OLMSTEAD
60
ORANGE
11
ORR
61, 63, 70, 116

OVERBY
60
OVERTON
81, 117

P

PAGE
54
PARK
87
PARKS
69
PATRICK
45, 71, 91
PATTERSON
37, 44, 45, 60, 71, 76, 133
PAYNE
2, 4, 5, 6, 7, 10, 11, 12, 14, 16, 32, 35, 37, 40, 45, 46, 51, 61, 70, 74, 76, 80, 81, 82, 85, 89, 94, 96, 98
PENA
26
PENICK
47, 51, 54, 55, 69, 115
PENNINGTON
60
PENNYCUFF
60
PEPPER
82
PERRY
57
PETERS
38, 59, 109
PETRIE
40, 98, 104
PETTY
60
PHILLIPS
15, 20, 28, 42
POE
11
POKE
98
PORTER
28, 34, 60, 75
POST
76

POWELL
17, 31, 96
PULLEY
27

Q

QUIN
76

R

RADFORD
18, 85
RAGER
17, 31, 40
RAMEY
92
RAMSEY
57
RANBURGER
96
RANDELL
26
RANDLE
112
REASON
46
REASONS
4, 80
REDFORD
106
REDING
115
REED
25
REEVES
60
REID
26
RICE
19
RIGGINS
78
ROBERTS
78, 81, 85
ROBERTSON
26, 27, 34, 42, 81
ROBEY
16, 21, 116
ROE
57

ROGERS
7, 69, 76, 102, 106
ROOSEVELT
76
ROSE
80
ROSSON
79
ROUSH
41
ROUTTE
53
ROYSTER
60
RUSSELL
19, 112
RUST
34, 40, 95, 102
RUTLEDGE
8, 38, 69, 89
RYALS
5, 8, 10, 14, 25, 26, 43, 56, 61, 69, 70

S

SADLER
46, 49, 70, 92, 133
SANDERS
32, 62, 63, 64, 74, 87, 100
SCHUERMAN
76
SCOTT
34, 36, 40, 69, 71, 126
SEARS
25, 40
SEAY
10, 26, 33, 39, 49, 51, 55, 65, 69, 71, 77, 78
SEAYS
9
SEBREE
83
SELF
70
SERVICE
38
SETTLE
106
SEVANN
69

SHACKELFORD
39
SHANKLIN
33, 40, 64
SHELTON
22, 113
SHEMWELL
116
SHEPHERD
21
SHEPPARD
40
SHERROD
97, 127
SHIRLEY
76
SHOLAR
53
SHORT
40, 94
SHOWERS
4, 10, 16
SHOWLEY
40
SHUMATE
31
SIMMONS
39, 71, 77
SIMONS
64
SIMPKINS
64
SIMPSON
8, 91
SIMS
76
SISK
25, 69, 89
SLACK
69
SLAUGHTER
116
SMALL
32, 79
SMITH
7, 8, 12, 19, 22, 25, 27, 35, 39, 43, 44, 45, 51, 58, 69, 71, 72, 74, 76, 78, 81, 83, 92, 112

SNADON
11, 13, 14, 76, 83
SNEAD
80
SNEED
116, 123
SNYDER
34
SOLOMON
109
SOUTHERN
76
SPENCER
18, 53, 54, 100, 103
SPOTTSWOOD
105
SPURLIN
30
STABLES
48
STAHL
4, 6, 7, 18, 20, 33, 38, 44, 47, 60, 69, 72
STARBIRD
19
STATTON
40
STINSON
92
STOCKWELL
108
STOKES
40, 78, 80
STRATTON
11, 61, 95, 116
STREET
41
SULLIVAN
26, 74, 76
SUMMERS
76
SUMPTER
81, 133
SWEENEY
35, 61, 63, 64, 70, 96, 132
SYDNOR
74
SZALAY
53

T

TANDY
112

TATUM
80

TAYLOR
12, 29, 30, 46, 58, 63, 69, 76, 78, 85

TEETER
92

TEMPLE
76

TEMPLEMAN
34, 40, 95, 96, 97

THOMAS
40, 81

THOMPSON
37, 41, 55, 71, 76, 85, 119

TILLIS
56

TOMERLIN
60

TOMLINSON
14

TREVENA
56

TRIBBLE
40, 44, 50, 64, 72, 76

TRICE
114

TROUTT
60

TURNER
34, 60, 78, 81

TYLER
69

U

UNDERWOOD
37

V

VAN METER
32, 35

VAUGHN
69, 116

VERNON
45, 77

VINSON
85, 89

W

WAGGONER
78

WALLER
35, 65, 74, 106, 132

WALLKER
60

WALTERS
24, 32

WALTON
60, 82

WARE
19, 45, 57, 77, 78, 85, 90, 99

WARFIELD
74

WARREN
69, 76, 110

WATSON
40

WATTS
17, 21, 26, 27, 41, 50, 64, 65, 69, 77, 78, 88, 90

WEATHERFORD
11, 71, 83, 132

WEATHERS
51, 57, 74, 121

WELBORN
8, 11, 36, 41, 98

WELLS
10, 40, 69

WEST
92

WESTERMAN
69

WHEELER
26, 28, 80

WHETSEL
41

WHITAKER
120, 127

WHITE
25, 26, 48, 83, 92, 94

WHITFIELD
38

WIECK
47

WILES
92

WILKINS
8, 15, 16, 17, 19, 60, 61, 81, 96

WILLIAMS
19, 36, 38, 41, 44, 57, 58, 59, 62, 65, 69, 76, 79, 81, 88, 106, 108, 125, 132

WILLIS
36, 61

WILSON
70, 81, 99

WINDERS
64

WOLFE
9, 60, 116

WOLFF
38

WOODALL
2, 44, 50, 59, 77, 85, 88, 89, 101

WOODS
40, 49, 77, 78, 101

WRIGHT
36, 53, 60, 87, 100, 111, 115, 116

WRIGHTS
88

WYATE
69

WYATT
12, 14, 15, 93

WYMAN
69

Y

YOST
82

YOUNG
54, 57, 70, 116

Leo Haley, owner and operator of Haley's Furniture Store on the square in Elkton, KY

Printed in the USA
CPSIA information can be obtained
at www.ICGtesting.com
LVHW081150080824
787694LV00006B/527